The Mexican War of Independence

Titles in the World History Series

WORLD HISTORY SERIES ■ ■ ■

The Mexican War of Independence

Lucent Books, P.O. Box 289011, San Diego, CA 92198-9011

Library of Congress Cataloging-in-Publication Data

The Mexican war of independence.
        p. cm. — (World history series)
    Includes bibliographical references (p.   ) and index.
Summary: Examines the events and legacy of Mexico's war of
independence from Spain.
    ISBN 1-56006-297-5
    1. Mexico—History—Wars of Independence, 1810–1821—
Juvenile literature. 2. Mexico—History—Juvenile literature.
[1. Mexico—History—Wars of Independence, 1810–1821.]
I. Series.
F1232.M49   1997
972'.03—dc20
                                                    96-14216
                                                      CIP
                                                       AC

Contents

Foreword

Each year on the first day of school, nearly every history teacher faces the task of explaining why his or her students should study history. One logical answer to this question is that exploring what happened in our past explains how the things we often take for granted—our customs, ideas, and institutions—came to be. As statesman and historian Winston Churchill put it, "Every nation or group of nations has its own tale to tell. Knowledge of the trials and struggles is necessary to all who would comprehend the problems, perils, challenges, and opportunities which confront us today." Thus, a study of history puts modern ideas and institutions in perspective. For example, though the founders of the United States were talented and creative thinkers, they clearly did not invent the concept of democracy. Instead, they adapted some democratic ideas that had originated in ancient Greece and with which the Romans, the British, and others had experimented. An exploration of these cultures, then, reveals their very real connection to us through institutions that continue to shape our daily lives.

Another reason often given for studying history is the idea that lessons exist in the past from which contemporary societies can benefit and learn. This idea, although controversial, has always been an intriguing one for historians. Those that agree that society can benefit from the past often quote philosopher George Santayana's famous statement, "Those who cannot remember the past are condemned to repeat it." Historians who ascribe to Santayana's philosophy believe that, for example, studying the events that led up to the major world wars or other significant historical events would allow society to chart a different and more favorable course in the future.

Just as difficult as convincing students to realize the importance of studying history is the search for useful and interesting supplementary materials that present historical events in a context that can be easily understood. The volumes in Lucent Books' World History Series attempt to present a broad, balanced, and penetrating view of the march of history. Ancient Egypt's important wars and rulers, for example, are presented against the rich and colorful backdrop of Egyptian religious, social, and cultural developments. The series engages the reader by enhancing historical events with these cultural contexts. For example, in *Ancient Greece*, the text covers the role of women in that society. Slavery is discussed in *The Roman Empire*, as well as how slaves earned their freedom. The numerous and varied aspects of everyday life in these and other societies are explored in each volume of the series. Additionally, the series covers the major political, cultural, and philosophical ideas as the torch of civilization is passed from ancient Mesopotamia and Egypt, through Greece, Rome, Medieval Europe, and other world cultures, to the modern day.

The material in the series is formatted in a thorough, precise, and organized manner. Each volume offers the reader a comprehensive and clearly written overview of an important historical event or period. The topic under discussion is placed in a broad historical context. For example, *The Italian Renaissance* begins with a discussion of the High Middle Ages and the loss of central control that allowed certain Italian cities to develop artistically. The book ends by looking forward to the Reformation and interpreting the societal changes that grew out of the Renaissance. Thus, students are not only involved in an historical era, but also enveloped by the events leading up to that era and the events following it.

One important and unique feature in the World History Series is the primary and secondary source quotations that richly supplement each volume. These quotes are useful in a number of ways. First, they allow students access to sources they would not normally be exposed to because of the difficulty and obscurity of the original source. The quotations range from interesting anecdotes to farsighted cultural perspectives and are drawn from historical witnesses both past and present. Second, the quotes demonstrate how and where historians themselves derive their information on the past as they strive to reach a consensus on historical events. Lastly, all of the quotes are footnoted, familiarizing students with the citation process and allowing them to verify quotes and/or look up the original source if the quote piques their interest.

Finally, the books in the World History Series provide a detailed launching point for further research. Each book contains a bibliography specifically geared toward student research. A second, annotated bibliography introduces students to all the sources the author consulted when compiling the book. A chronology of important dates gives students an overview, at a glance, of the topic covered. Where applicable, a glossary of terms is included.

In short, the series is designed not only to acquaint readers with the basics of history, but also to make them aware that their lives are a part of an ongoing human saga. Perhaps they will then come to the same realization as famed historian Arnold Toynbee. In his monumental work, *A Study of History*, he wrote about becoming aware of history flowing through him in a mighty current, and of his own life "welling like a wave in the flow of this vast tide."

Important Dates in the History of the Mexican War of Independence

ca.1519	1810	1811	1813	1814	1815	1821–1822	1823	1829	183

1519
Cortés invades Mexico and claims it for Spain; "New Spain" is finally established in 1535, but Indian resistance and rebellions continue throughout three centuries of colonial rule

1810
El Grito de Dolores: The *grito*, or call to action, that began the revolution that would end in Mexican independence from Spain

1811
Hidalgo is captured and executed; the revolution continues with southern troops led by Father José María Morelos y Pavón

1813
Congress of Chilpancingo formally declares independence from Spain and sets out the principles of government for the new nation

1814
Decreto de Apatzingán sets out a plan for governing Mexico

1815
Morelos is captured and executed; the revolution continues with guerrilla warfare led by Nicolás Bravo, Vicente Guerrero, and Guadalupe Victoria

1821–1822
Agustín de Iturbide joins in the battle for independence from Spain; after independence is won, the original revolutionaries are shut out as the military supports Iturbide's declaration that he will rule Mexico as an emperor

1823
Military officer Antonio López de Santa Anna deposes the emperor and Mexico is declared a republic; Santa Anna is in and out of power for the next three decades; by one count, he holds the presidency eleven times

1829
Spain tries unsuccessfully to recapture Mexico

1836
Texas declares its independence from Mexico; Santa Anna's army defeats Texans at the Alamo

1838
France invades Veracruz in so-called Pastry War

1846–1848
Mexican-American War; with Treaty of Guadalupe Hildalgo, Mexico cedes nearly half of its territory to the United States

1855–1861
Santa Anna's long career ends with revolution; during La Reforma, land is distributed to the poor and the power of the church is limited; Benito Juárez and Liberals maintain power through bloody two-year civil war

1862
Supported by England and Spain, France invades Mexico; French troops march triumphantly into Mexico City and install a French emperor, Maximilian

1867
Juárez drives out the French and Maximilian, ending the last foreign government of Mexico

1876
Porfirio Díaz seizes power; he will rule the country until 1911, in a dictatorship known as the Porfiriato

1910
Mexican Revolution begins; leaders Francisco Madero, Pancho Villa, and Emiliano Zapata are all eventually assassinated, but conflict ends with successful establishment of a new constitution in 1917

1934–1940
President Lázaro Cárdenas implements many of the reforms on behalf of the poor for which the country's earlier revolutionaries—Hidalgo, Juárez, and Zapata—fought and died

1994
A new revolutionary group, the Zapatista National Liberation Army (EZLN), initiates guerrilla warfare in Chiapas, declaring its intention to fight for the rights of Indians, peasants, and other poor people; within weeks, EZLN and government begin peace talks

Independence and Justice: A Continuing Struggle

The Mexican War of Independence was fought to win freedom from Spain and equal rights for all races and classes of people. Winning independence was the easier part of the battle. The struggle for equality and justice was, and is, much more difficult.

The original Mexican revolutionaries were split in their goals. On one side, wealthy Creoles, natives of European descent, wanted to replace the Spanish colonial rulers by seizing power for themselves. They were not opposed to the control of the government and the wealth of the

Father Miguel Hidalgo y Costilla, known as the father of Mexican independence, led Mexico's struggle for freedom from Spain.

MEXICO

country by a small elite—they just wanted to throw out the Spanish and become that elite themselves. They did not want to share either power or wealth with the poor.

On the other side, masses of poor Indians and mestizos, of mixed European and Indian blood, led by Father Miguel Hidalgo y Costilla, also wanted to throw out the Spaniards, but their goals encompassed more: They wanted dignity, justice, and land of their own.

Led by Hidalgo, the father of Mexican independence, the masses swept over Mexico like an uncontrollable fire during the first year of the war. Lacking guns to meet the Spanish soldiers, tens of thousands died, using sheer numbers to overcome the firepower of the military. When the tide of the war turned, Hidalgo was captured and executed.

Others continued the struggle for independence. Gradually, the colonial government conquered most of the rebellious armies. The independence fighters retreated to the mountains or disappeared back into their communities. Sporadic guerrilla warfare continued.

A decade after Hidalgo's execution, one of the army officers who had fought against the revolution decided that he would fight for independence. Agustín de Iturbide won the independence of Mexico from Spain, but he also crushed the revolutionary dreams that began the war for independence. Instead of sharing power with the poor, he made himself an emperor and preserved the wealth and control of the privileged classes. As one twentieth-century activist writes, Iturbide wanted a "Revolution for Independence and Privilege, as opposed to the people's Revolution for Independence and the Land."[1]

Although Iturbide won independence from Spain, neither the fight for independence nor the revolutionary battle of the poor ended with him. Foreign countries eager for land or resources still threatened Mexico's independence: years of armed conflict remained before Spain, France, England, and the United States agreed to leave Mexico alone.

And within Mexico, revolutionaries continued to fight for equal rights and for redistribution of wealth using both political and military means. Race was a significant issue for the first revolutionaries, and has continued to be an issue in each of Mexico's revolutionary struggles. Since the conquest of the Aztecs by Spanish invading armies, native peoples have been oppressed. Even today, they suffer from poverty and discrimination.

Land, too, is a major issue in Mexico. Hidalgo's revolutionaries wanted to redistribute the land that had been seized by the Spanish invaders, returning some to Indians and to others who actually farmed the land. That goal was part of the continuing revolutionary programs of Benito Juárez in 1857, of Emiliano Zapata in 1910, of Lázaro Cárdenas in 1934, and of the Zapatista rebels in 1994.

Each new wave of Mexican revolutionaries has claimed the heritage of those who have gone before. Revolution is part of the political culture of Mexico, reflected even in the name of the political party continuously in power for the past sixty years, the Institutional Revolutionary Party, or PRI.

Today in Mexico struggles between rich and poor continue. Just as in 1810, ownership and distribution of land is a major issue. Race and racism both shape and distort Mexican culture and politics. Nationalism is both a source of pride and a barrier to international cooperation. Studying the Mexican War of Independence can help us to understand the conflicts Mexico faces as it approaches the twenty-first century.

Chapter

1 Prelude: Conquest and Resistance

When Hernando Cortés and his Spanish conquistadores arrived in Mexico in 1519, they were looking for gold. They also intended to claim the territory for Spain, to convert any inhabitants to Christianity, and to gain wealth, property, and power for themselves and their descendants.

Neither the Aztec elite nor the subject communities knew what to make of Cortés. Was he a foreign invader? Or could he be Quetzalcoatl, the god who many years before had promised to return, coming from the east?

Communication was difficult, since neither side knew the language of the other. The initial native reaction was resistance. In one of Cortés's first encounters, the Tabascan Indian chiefs launched an army of twelve thousand against the Spanish invaders, but the Tabascan army proved no match for the Spaniards' vastly superior weaponry and firepower. When the entire Tabascan force was defeated by four hundred Spaniards, caciques (chiefs) from Tabasco and neighboring towns tried to appease the Spaniards with gifts of food, quilted cotton material, gold ornaments, and twenty slave women.

Among the women was Malinche, a fifteen-year-old princess who had been

Malinche stands at Cortés's side, interpreting the language of Aztec prisoners. Malinche's ability to interpret the language and behavior of the Aztecs was invaluable to Cortés.

Accompanied by native allies, Cortés and his cavalry march across the causeway leading into the Aztec capital, Tenochtitlán.

sold into slavery. She spoke both her native Nahuatl and the Mayan language of her Tabascan owners. Quickly converting to Christianity and learning Spanish, Malinche became Cortés's translator. The role of Malinche, known after her baptism as Doña Marina, is described in *Ten Notable Women of Latin America:*

> The story of the conquest is one of the most incredible in American history. Cortés the conquistador and Montezuma the emperor soon confronted each other at the gates of the Aztec capital. The date was November 8, 1519. Their encounter was the first act of a drama that would soon destroy one of them and immortalize them both. And standing at the side of the Spaniard was a third figure—that of the Indian woman Malinche.
>
> History . . . has largely overlooked her as a striking personality in her own right—someone without whom Cortés surely would have failed to defeat Montezuma and the Aztecs by 1521.[2]

Malinche eased communication for the Spaniards, who hoped to gain more information about the gold and silver ornaments that the Aztecs offered them. The ornaments proved that there was gold and silver in Mexico. Bernal Díaz del Castillo, one of Cortés's soldiers, later wrote a history of the conquest. He described gifts sent by Montezuma, the Aztec *huery-tlatoani*, or emperor, to the approaching Spaniards:

> The first article presented was a wheel like a sun, as big as a cartwheel, with many sorts of pictures on it, the whole of fine gold, and a wonderful thing to behold, which those who afterwards weighed it said was worth more than ten thousand dollars. Then another wheel was presented of greater size made of silver of great brilliancy in imitation of the moon with other figures shown on it, and this was of great value as it was very heavy—and the chief brought back the helmet full of fine grains of gold, just as they are got out of the mines, and this was worth

The Arrival of Cortés

According to Howard Zinn in A People's History of the United States, *the Aztecs were not sure whether to do battle with Cortés as an invader or to welcome him as a friend or even a god.*

"The Aztec civilization of Mexico came out of the heritage of the Mayan, Zapotec, and Toltec cultures. It built enormous constructions from stone tools and human labor, developed a writing system and a priesthood. It also engaged in (let us not overlook this) the ritual killing of thousands of people as sacrifices to the gods. The cruelty of the Aztecs, however, did not erase a certain innocence, and when a Spanish armada appeared at Vera Cruz, and a bearded white man came ashore, . . . it was thought that he was the legendary Aztec man-god who had died three hundred years before, with the promise to return—the mysterious Quetzalcoatl. And so they welcomed him, with munificent hospitality.

That was Hernando Cortés, come from Spain with . . . one obsessive goal: to find gold. In the mind of Montezuma, the king of the Aztecs, there must have been a certain doubt about whether Cortés was indeed Quetzalcoatl, because he sent a hundred runners to Cortés, bearing enormous treasures, gold and silver wrought into objects of fantastic beauty, but at the same time begging him to go back. . . .

Cortés then began his march of death from town to town, using deception, turning Aztec against Aztec, killing with the kind of deliberateness that accompanies a strategy—to paralyze the will of the population by a sudden frightful deed. And so, in Cholulu, he invited the headmen of the Cholula nation to the square. And when they came, with thousands of unarmed retainers, Cortés's small army of Spaniards, posted around the square with cannon, armed with crossbows, mounted on horses, massacred them, down to the last man. Then they looted the city and moved on. When their cavalcade of murder was over they were in Mexico City, Montezuma was dead, and the Aztec civilization, shattered, was in the hands of the Spaniards.

All this is told in the Spaniards' own accounts."

three thousand dollars. This gold in the helmet was worth more to us than if it had contained twenty thousand dollars, because it showed us that there were good mines there. Then were brought twenty golden ducks, beautifully worked and very natural looking, and some [ornaments] like dogs, and many articles of gold worked in the shape of tigers and lions and monkeys, and ten collars beautifully worked and other necklaces; and twelve arrows and a bow with its string, and two rods like staffs of justice, five palms long, all in beautiful hollow work of fine gold.[3]

Believing that Cortés might be the god Quetzalcoatl, the great sixteenth-century Aztec emperor Montezuma (pictured) failed to resist the Spanish invaders.

The conquering Spaniards occupied the Aztec capital, Tenochtitlán, and took Montezuma captive. They demanded more gold, submission of the people to Spanish rule, and conversion of the Aztecs to the Christian religion, beginning with Montezuma. Although he eventually gave in to the other demands, Montezuma refused to renounce his religion, and died in custody. The Aztec armies fought back, eventually driving the Spaniards from the city. A year later, however, Cortés returned to Tenochtitlán to do battle against the new Aztec leader, Cuauhtémoc.

This time the city of Tenochtitlán was taken apart by the invaders. The Spaniards filled in its aqueduct and canals, destroyed its fruitful island gardens. When the people of Tenochtitlán still resisted, the Spanish soldiers laid siege to the city, starving many of its inhabitants. In house-to-house combat, they slaughtered others. Cuauhtémoc himself was taken captive and later killed.

The conquest of the Aztecs, whose empire comprised the regions around present-day Mexico City, was completed in 1521, but other parts of Mexico remained independent for decades. The Mixtón War broke out in 1541 in the western territory between Jalisco and Zacatecas. In this conflict, Indians who remained loyal to their traditional religions burned Christian churches and destroyed monasteries in an attempt to rid Mexico of Catholicism and the Spaniards. Mayans rebelled in the south in 1546, in another indigenous religious movement. Mayan priests led the effort to cleanse their society of all that came from Spain, even horses, cows, pigs, and European grain. These revolts delayed complete conquest of the Mayan part of Mexico until 1547.

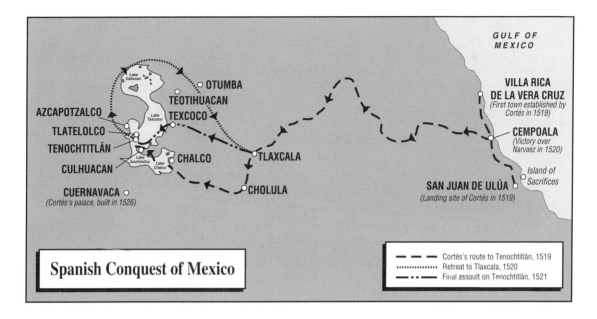

Spanish Conquest of Mexico

Cortés's route to Tenochtitlán, 1519
Retreat to Tlaxcala, 1520
Final assault on Tenochtitlán, 1521

Spanish Rule

Spain named its conquered territory New Spain. Now that Mexico was a Spanish colony, the Spanish monarchs were the legal owners of all the land in Mexico: They alone controlled trade and collected taxes. Though Mexico had been conquered by soldiers and adventurers, Spain did not allow them to rule its new territory. Mexico was governed by a viceroy sent from Spain, who reported directly to the Spanish monarch.

The monarchy also sent *visitadores* to monitor the performance of the viceroy and to report back to the king. A further check on the power of the viceroy came from *audiencias*. These regional courts of review were headed by *oidores*, or judges. *Audiencias* were technically answerable to the viceroy, legal arms of his administration. In practice, however, some *audiencias* ruled various parts of Mexico. Other local units of government existed as well. A city

might be governed by an alcalde, or mayor. A state or province might have its own *gobernador*, or governor. A great bureaucracy of officials was appointed by Spain. In theory, all were answerable to the viceroy and, ultimately, to the Spanish king or queen. In practice, they often operated with considerable independence.

This complex government structure reinforced a rigid class system based on race. Each class of people was given a different legal status and different legal privileges. European-born Spaniards, called *peninsulares*, remained at the top of the hierarchy. They comprised about 10,000 of a total Mexican population of more than 5 million. Two-thirds of a million Creoles, or Mexican-born Spaniards, made up the next level in the legally and socially stratified society. Mestizo descendants of Spanish-Indian parents occupied a lower rung on the social ladder. Mestizos made up about 1.5 million of the population. At the bottom, oppressed and in some cases virtually enslaved, were the more than 2.5

Tenochtitlán: City in a Lake

"As its power and importance increased, [Tenochtitlán] was quickly transformed from a village of reed huts into an imperial capital covering nearly five square miles. Because of its island locality, land was scarce and the Aztecs were forced to drain the surrounding swamps in order to provide more building land and garden plots. Canals were cut through the reed beds, and the debris piled up between the canals to make artificial platforms. Alternate layers of mud and reeds were added to raise the level, and the platforms were consolidated by driving in wickerwork hurdles around the sides and by planting trees whose roots anchored the platforms to the lake bottom. . . .

Sealed off behind [a ten-mile-long] dike, Tenochtitlán stood like a Mexican Venice in an artificial lagoon fed by streams of fresh water. Causeways linked the city with the mainland and aqueducts carried water from springs on the shore. A grid of canals reached to all parts of Tenochtitlán, dividing it into rectangular blocks."

The magnificent city of Tenochtitlán as it may have appeared before its destruction by Spanish conquerors.

million Indians and blacks, both slave and free, and their descendants.

Land Ownership

Land was also administered strictly under Spanish rule. Spain granted parcels called *encomiendas* as rewards for services rendered, as signs of royal favor, or as tribute to the church. The *encomendero*, or title-holder, received the right not only to the land but also to the labor of the Indians living there. Though the land was still technically owned by the king or queen of Spain, the *encomendero* had absolute power over the Indians, though he had to pay a percentage of his profits to the Spanish Crown.

Cortés was among those Spaniards that received *encomiendas*. He was initially given rights to the labor of twenty-three thousand Indians, and later surreptitiously increased the number to fifty thousand.

In theory, the Spanish conquerors and *encomenderos* were supposed to educate the Indians and convert them to Christianity. They saw themselves as enlightened, bringing civilization and Christianity to savages. In practice, Spanish power could itself be quite savage. Mexican historian Ramón Eduardo Ruiz describes the operation of the well-established *encomienda* system:

> The Indian was compelled to work for Spaniards unwilling to till the land, forced to supply parasitical men with food, clothing, and shelter. So began the exploitation of the "bronze" man by the white, the subjugation of one race to another, the New World by the Old. Ironically, the law judged encomienda Indians "free men" because

they were not slaves. Theory and fact stood at opposite poles.

> . . . Encomenderos, first off, had their pick of the Indian women, whether with husband or not. They used them as domestics and as concubines and, when they were no longer useful, drove them away. On the sugar plantations, the encomenderos "married" them off to their slaves. Some beat their Indians to death; others buried them alive; the less cruel killed them with guns. . . . The best of the encomenderos drove their Indians from dawn to dusk, while the heartless robbed them of their goods. [4]

The *encomienda* farms and mines furnished agricultural produce and mineral wealth to the mother country of Spain. Other benefits came in less direct ways. Spain could and did prohibit Mexico from producing crops or goods that competed with Spanish products. Only the mother country was allowed to produce wine, for example. In the colonial tradition, Spain both collected taxes from Mexico and controlled Mexico's trade for Spain's benefit. For the most part, Mexico was not allowed to trade with other countries. Spain could demand all of its exports, its entire silver production, for example, "purchased" at prices set arbitrarily low.

And Spain could and did demand that Mexico import products only from Spain. Spanish manufacturers decreed that they alone could supply Mexico, even if the same goods were available at lower prices from England or its American colonies.

> [T]extile barons and merchants in Seville persuaded Spanish authorities to bar colonial enterprise, and,

Conquest Means Death

In The Discovery and Conquest of Mexico, *Bernal Díaz del Castillo describes his experiences in the battle for Tenochtitlán.*

"We knew already that the Indians in the city were much discouraged, and we heard from two wretched Indians who had left the city by night and come to our camp that the people were dying of hunger and that they came out by night to search among the houses and in those parts of the city we had already captured, seeking for firewood and herbs and roots for food. As we had already filled in many of the canals and made good many of the bad places I decided to enter the city before dawn and do all the damage we were able, so the launches set out before daybreak, and I with twelve or fifteen horsemen and some foot soldiers and allies entered with a rush, but first of all while we were in hiding we stationed some spies who as soon as day dawned gave us the signal to advance, and we fell on a great multitude of people, but as they were the poor wretches who had come out hunting for food they were most of them unarmed and were women and children, and we did so much damage to them whenever we could get about the city that prisoners and dead between them numbered eight hundred.

The launches also captured many canoes with Indians who were out fishing. When the captains and chieftains of the enemy saw us advancing through the city at this unusual hour they were dismayed, and did not dare to come out and fight us, so we returned to our camp with booty and food for our allies."

Spanish invaders and their Indian allies clash with Aztec warriors.

Spanish priest Bartolomé de Las Casas, an advocate for the rights of Indians, denounced the practice of converting non-Christians by force.

consequently, manufacturing in New Spain received a severe setback. . . .

Relying on the Casa de Contratación, authorities watched over commerce. Their goal was to aid Spanish merchants, whose goods arrived by way of a fleet sailing annually from Seville, carrying wines and perfumes as well as steel, iron tools, hats, and the like for the well-off. The royal treasury taxed almost everything sold in New Spain; one tax, the *alcabala*, grew rapidly over the years. These policies stifled commerce and industry, driving prices up and encouraging colonials, again and again, to buy contraband goods.[5]

While Spain was the official and most visible ruling power in Mexico, another great power stood alongside the viceroy and the political system: the Roman Catholic Church. The church was intertwined with civil government, working closely with it at all levels. Local priests collected fees amounting to taxes from their towns. Some fees were paid to the church by the town itself, such as a fee for a bishop's visit. Others were collected from families in need of religious services such as baptisms, weddings, or funerals.

Religion and Rule

Church doctrine permeated all civil actions by the Spaniards. Spaniards believed that, as Christians, God gave them and their king rights over all non-Christian peoples. Spanish priests and soldiers told Indians that they must be baptized and become Christians. Frequently, those who refused were killed. Like the traders who bought and sold African slaves, the Spaniards regarded Indians as less than human. They claimed a God-given right to the land, property, and labor of the Indians. A Spanish priest, Juan Ginés de Sepúlveda, argued strongly for this viewpoint. As historian Lewis Hanke reports, Sepúlveda declared Indians to be as inferior

as children are to adults, as women are to men. Indians are as different from

Spaniards believed that it was their duty to bring Christianity to the Indians. Here, a priest orders Spanish soldiers to tear down a Mexican idol.

Spaniards as cruel people are from mild people.

Compare then those blessings enjoyed by Spaniards of prudence, genius, magnanimity, temperance, humanity, and religion with those of the homunculi [little men] in whom you will scarcely find even vestiges of humanity, who not only possess no science but who also lack letters and preserve no monument of their history except certain vague and obscure reminiscences of some things in certain paintings. Neither do they have written laws, but bar-baric institutions and customs. They do not even have private property.[6]

Not all clergymen agreed with this line of reasoning. Some, like Bartolomé de Las Casas, were strong advocates for the rights of Indians. In his manifesto *The Devastation of the Indies, A Brief Account*, Las Casas documented atrocities committed by the conquerors.

Thus, from the beginning of their discovery of New Spain, that is to say, from the eighteenth of April in the year one thousand five hundred and eighteen until the year thirty, a period of twelve whole years, there were continual massacres and outrages committed by the bloody hands and swords of the Spaniards against the Indians living on the four hundred and fifty leagues of land surrounding the city of Mexico [Tenochtitlán], which comprised four or five great kingdoms as large as and more felicitous than Spain. Those lands were all more densely populated than Toledo or Seville and Valladolid and Zaragoza all combined, along with Barcelona. Never has there been such a population as in these cities which God saw fit to place in that vast expanse of land having a circumference of more than a thousand leagues. The Spaniards have killed more Indians here in twelve years by the sword, by fire, and enslavement than anywhere else in the Indies. They have killed young and old, men, women, and children, some four million souls during what they call the Conquests, which were the violent invasions of cruel tyrants that should be condemned not only by the law of God but by all the laws of man. . . . And this does not take into account those Indians who have died from ill treatment or were killed under tyrannical servitude.[7]

Las Casas and his followers believed in conversion of the Indians to Christianity, but only by peaceful persuasion.

Las Casas and other clergy who advocated for the Indians frequently found themselves threatened by and in trouble with both governmental and religious authority. *Encomenderos* angered by their preaching sometimes threatened physical violence against the priests. Some schools founded for Indians were forced to close. One formal response to Las Casas's *The Devastation of the Indies* shows the degree of anger against defenders of Indians in its title: *Against the premature, scandalous and heretical assertions which Fray Bartolomé de las Casas has made in his book about the conquest of the Indies, which he has had printed without permission of the authorities.*

Willingly or not, many Indians did convert to Christianity. At times, their traditional customs and religious practices were merged with Christian practices. For example, devotion to Christian saints frequently incorporated elements of the age-old religious veneration of Mayan or Aztec gods. One example became the single most important symbol drawing Indians to the church: the Virgin of Guadalupe.

In 1531, an Indian by the name of Juan Diego saw a vision of a woman on a mountainside. The woman, clothed in traditional Indian dress, identified herself as the Blessed Virgin Mary, the mother of Jesus and the most revered woman in Christian tradition. This lady, however, had dark skin, hair, and eyes, resembling the poor Indians of Mexico rather than the Spanish elite. Various elements of her dress seemed to identify the lady as the intermediary between the Aztec religion and the new age to come. This appearance of the Blessed Virgin Mary became known as the Virgin of Guadalupe or Our Lady of Guadalupe.

The Virgin of Guadalupe became the most revered religious icon of Mexico and of all Latin America. She was seen as a sign that God and the Virgin would speak to and take the side of the poor and oppressed Indian people. When the War of Independence began, Mexicans marched under the banner of the Virgin of Guadalupe, claiming her as their leader in revolution.

Genocide

The Spanish priest Bartolomé de Las Casas observed and described many of the horrors of the conquest in The Devastation of the Indies, A Brief Account.

"Among other massacres there was the one in a big city of more than thirty thousand inhabitants, which is called Cholula. The people came out to welcome all the lords of the country and the earth. . . .

Soon after this the Spaniards agreed to carry out a massacre, or as they called it a punitive attack, in order to sow terror and apprehension, and to make a display of their power in every corner of that land. This was always the determination of the Spaniards in all the lands they conquered: to commit a great massacre that would terrorize the tame flock and make it tremble. . . .

When [five or six thousand Indians designated as burden-carriers for the Spaniards] were all placed close together they were bound and tied. At the closed doorways armed guards took turns to see that none escaped. Then at a command, all the Spaniards drew their swords or pikes and while their chiefs looked on, helpless, all those . . . were butchered, cut to pieces. . . . Then the Spaniards had the chiefs, a total of more than a hundred, who were already shackled, burned at the stakes that had been driven into the ground. . . .

The Christians (who know something of God and of reason and of human laws) should realize how astounding all this is to simple people, living peacefully on their lands and who have their own chiefs, to be told by the Spaniards of a new Spanish ruler never seen or heard of before, and that if they do not subject themselves to that King they will be cut to pieces. It makes their hearts stand still, for they have seen from experience that this will be done. And the most horrifying thing is that the Indians who do obey are placed in servitude where with incredible hard labor and torments even harder to endure and longer lasting than the torments of those who are put to the sword they are finally, with their wives and children and their whole generation, exterminated."

The Virgin of Guadalupe, a divine symbol of hope to the Indian people, is the most revered religious icon of Mexico.

Excluded from power and wealth, increasingly oppressed and impoverished, the Mexican majority was hardly content with its lot. As the eighteenth century gave way to the nineteenth, revolution was in the air around the world. The American Revolution united thirteen British colonies to the north of Mexico into a single nation, the United States of America. The grand revolutionary rhetoric of human equality and "certain unalienable Rights, [among them] Life, Liberty and the pursuit of Happiness" inspired hope in people far beyond the borders of the British colonies. The French Revolution in 1789 sounded an even clearer call: "Liberty! Equality! Fraternity!" To people deprived of liberty and oppressed by a colonial power, these two revolutions offered both hope and inspiration.

To the ruling classes and colonial powers, the two revolutions represented threats to order and morality. Kings were, after all, God's representatives on earth. How dare people reject their divinely appointed rulers? And if further evidence of the evil of revolution were needed, they could point to France, where revolutionary excesses washed the country in blood flowing from the guillotines. In Mexico, however, such cautions would not be heeded for long.

2 Father of Independence

Although the War of Independence was the work of masses of people, Miguel Hidalgo y Costilla became its focal point and is still known as the father of Mexican independence. The life of this Mexican leader, like the movement itself, had been affected by issues of race and class. Hidalgo's education and career options were wider than those of many others because he was born into a higher social class. As he grew older, Hidalgo studied revolutionary writers and ideas. As a teacher and a priest, he taught others about the ideals of freedom and equality. His students and friends came from many classes and walks of life, including Indians, Spanish government officials, and Creole army officers.

Hidalgo was born on May 8, 1753, the first child of Don Cristóbal Hidalgo y Costilla and Doña Ana María Gallaga Mandarte. Like her husband, Doña Ana María was a Creole, born in the part of Mexico now known as Michoacán and descended from the well-known Spanish families of Villaseñor, Silva, and Gallaga. Miguel's three full brothers, José Joaquin, Manuel Mariano, and José María were born within the next six years.

Hidalgo was born on the ranch of San Vicente, a part of the estate of Corralejos, where his father worked as manager, and where he met and married Doña Ana María Gallaga in 1752. Orphaned at an early age, she came to San Vicente to live with an uncle when she was about twenty years old.

Although he was an estate manager and not a landowner, Don Cristóbal was well-to-do. A 1764 inventory reveals that he owned 338 head of cattle, 4 horses, 5

Hidalgo's fight for social, political, and economic change made him a principal figure in the War of Independence.

Mexican natives gather in a hut to make tortillas. Hidalgo, whose teachings focused on issues of race and class, wanted to help Indians and mestizos gain the right to own land.

Negro and mulatto slaves, and a clavichord. The fact that he and his wife were called "Don" and "Doña" is also indicative of higher status, as these are terms of respect, something like "Sir" and "Madam."

Hidalgo's education began at home, where he was most likely privately tutored by a priest. Priests were frequently hired as teachers by families with enough money to educate their children, for public education as it exists today was unknown in Mexico in the eighteenth century. When Miguel was twelve, he and his brother José Joaquin were sent to a Jesuit-run college in the town of Valladolid about sixty-five miles southeast of their home.

In their youths, Hidalgo and his brothers lived through dramatic political developments that allowed them expanded opportunities. When Carlos III became

During his reign, Spanish king Carlos III granted Creoles expanded rights in New Spain, a move that angered many Spanish-born residents of Mexico.

king of Spain in 1759, his Bourbon reforms allowed Creoles expanded political rights in New Spain. For the first time Creoles were allowed to enter colleges and universities and have careers in law and in the church. Even some lower government offices were opened to them.

The Spanish-born residents of Mexico fought against these reforms. They were not ready to share their privileged position with their Mexican-born relatives.

When Carlos IV became king of Spain in 1788, he began to reverse the reforms of his father, restricting Creole rights again, strengthening the *peninsulares* and creating resentment among Creoles who had tasted the possibility of equality.

> Believing *peninsulares* more loyal than criollos [Creoles], the crown reserved for them two-thirds of all posts on the ayuntamientos [municipal governments] and audiencias; by 1790, for example, just three of the eleven *oidores* of the audiencia of Mexico City were criollos. . . . From the perspective of the criollos, the Bourbons had sabotaged their political aspirations and, by reserving important public jobs for *peninsulares*, confined them to the ones that paid poorly.[8]

Many Creoles lost hope for changing their situation. Among those disappointed Creoles was Miguel Hidalgo.

Hidalgo's Education and Early Career

The college that Hidalgo attended was run by Jesuit priests. The Jesuits, a society of priests that was not answerable to local bishops, were considered dangerously independent. Both local bishops and government officials suspected the well-educated Jesuits of subversive ideas and teaching. Two years after he arrived in Valladolid, Miguel's college was closed by the government, and its Jesuit teachers were arrested.

After his college was closed, Hidalgo transferred to the diocesan Colegio San Nicolás in the same city. The education in colleges managed by diocesan clergy was inferior to that provided by Jesuits.

An excellent student, Miguel was nicknamed *El Zorro* or "the Fox" by fellow students who admired his quick mind. Miguel's appetite for learning was not satisfied by the restricted offerings of his college. His reading went beyond the assigned books, including some authors and books that were actually forbidden by the church or government authorities.

The discrimination Hidalgo experienced as a Creole prompted him to study and think about its broader implications.

Trade in New Spain

Spain kept its colonies dependent on the mother country, prohibiting them from trading with other countries. This served to generate more wealth for Spain. William Davis Robinson, an observer from the United States, writes about trade in Memoirs of the Mexican Revolution.

"The commerce and agriculture of the Creoles have likewise felt the fatal and dreadful influence of Spanish despotism. The commerce of the colonies has been restricted to a few Cadiz merchants. The arts, exactions, and injustice, of these avaricious monopolists, would scarcely be believed by the civilized world. Our limits will not permit us to detail them, but we may observe, that extortion was the leading feature of that disgraceful commerce. The shipments to Mexico consisted of cargoes of the miserable manufactures of Spain, or, of the imperfect products of her agriculture, and of some foreign fabrics, so burthened with imposts, that only the most wealthy classes of society could buy them. The consumption of such cargoes was forced upon the Creoles, by a very arbitrary and ingenious measure, to the exclusion of commerce through any other channel but that of old Spain; and to the neglect of those advantages, which all-bountiful nature has granted the Americans, in the fertility of their soil, and genial climate. To ensure the sale of Spanish wines and brandies, the Creoles were forbidden to manufacture either; olives were not allowed to be planted; the cultivation of the silk worm was interdicted; and, with regard to vines, even such as had been raised for the purpose of affording the Creole a grateful fruit, became an object of jealousy to the Cadiz monopolists, and an order was actually sent out by the government of Spain, to grab up all the vines in the country."

Race and Class in New Spain

Lucas Alamán, a Mexican historian who lived through the War of Independence and later became a Conservative government official, wrote a three-volume history of the war, Historia de Méjico, desde los primeros movimientos que prepararon su independencia en el año de 1808 hasta la época presente. *His description of the definition of race illuminates the attitudes of the time.*

"The conquest introduced in the population of New Spain, and in general, of all the continent of America, other elements that it is indispensable to know, as much in their number as in their distribution over the topography of the country, because all of the circumstances, and even more the distinction that the laws made between diverse classes of inhabitants, were a great influence in the revolution and in all of the successive events. These new elements were Spaniards and the Negroes they brought from Africa. A short time later the Spaniards distinguished among themselves between those born in Europe and those native to America, to whom for this reason they gave the name of *criollos*, which came with the passing of time to be considered as an insult, though in its origin it signified no more than one born and raised in this land. From the mixture of Spaniards with the Indian class came the *mestizos*, just as from the mixture of all with the Negroes, the mullatos, zambos, pardos and all the varied nomenclature that is comprehended in the generic name of *castas*.

The children of Spaniards and Indians are called *mestizos*; of Spaniards and Negroes, *mulatos*; of Indians and Negroes, *zambos*, and as it is thought that Negro blood carries a taint of infamy more than all the rest, there are further strange categories that mark its persistence, by successive degrees of kinship, to the distance from the African origin. . . .

To the Spaniards born in Europe, whom I shall call only Europeans, was given the name of *gachupines*, which in the Mexican language signifies 'men who have shoes with points or which pick,' an allusion to the spurs, and this name, like that of creole, with the progress of rivalry between the one and the other, also came to be held as offensive."

From the writings of Bartolomé de Las Casas to the histories of the French and American Revolutions, his studies convinced him of the equality of persons and the injustice of the caste system of his country. Hidalgo grew up in a slaveholding household, but by the time he reached adulthood he was convinced that all people should be free.

In 1770, when he was seventeen, Hidalgo received a bachelor of arts degree. His degree was actually granted by the Royal and Pontifical University of Mexico in Mexico City rather than by the college he attended. Three years later, after continuing his studies, he earned the degree of bachelor of theology. Miguel and José Joaquin, who also attended the college of San Nicolás, were both ordained as priests. Miguel went on to teach at the college of San Nicolás Obispo; he became its rector in 1790.

His church salary was high enough to enable Don Miguel to buy two farms. After just two years as rector he resigned, however, and took a post as a parish priest in a distant town. José Joaquin took a position as parish priest in the small town of Dolores in 1794, a post he held until his death in 1803. Don Miguel frequently visited him, helping out with some of the church duties and becoming acquainted with the town and people of Dolores.

In about 1800 two priests, Fray Joaquin Huesca and Fray Manuel Estrada, filed serious accusations against Miguel Hidalgo, ranging from reading and teaching heresy to womanizing to carrying a copy of the Koran, the sacred book of Islam. The charges were presented to officials of the Holy Office, also known as the Inquisition.

The Holy Office was the Roman Catholic Church body that had jurisdiction to act on charges of heresy or offenses against the church. Luckily for Don Miguel, Fray Estrada was widely regarded as a habitual liar, and although the Inquisition did investigate the charges, its ac-

tions were comparatively moderate. During its investigation, the Holy Office interviewed at least thirteen other witnesses and recorded additional evidence for future reference that Don Miguel read forbidden books, including French literature, and that he seemed to hold revolutionary ideas.

Although the Inquisition entered no formal judgment against him, Don Miguel still lost his post as a parish priest in San Felipe. Until he took over the parish in Dolores after José Joaquin's death, Don Miguel had no regular employment.

Parish Priest in Dolores

As a priest in Dolores, Hidalgo baptized, married, and buried people from every level of society. In addition to his religious duties he began working with Indians at Dolores, encouraging them to become economically self-sufficient. Hidalgo's projects were motivated by a deep-seated commitment to the social, economic, and political reform of an unjust society. According to Hidalgo biographer Arthur Noll, Hidalgo

taught the Indians the art of tanning hides, and so enabled them to produce leather at a much lower cost than they were accustomed to pay for it when bought of the Spanish merchants. He established a factory in which he introduced better methods of making the earthenware than the Indians had used before the Conquest; and he taught them how to make better bricks than the sun-dried

Hidalgo preached the ideals of freedom and equality to his Indian congregation.

adobes which they had been accustomed to make. . . . In few words, he was fitting the Indians of his neighborhood to pursue the occupations of free people rather than those of slaves.[9]

Among Hidalgo's first projects were planting mulberry trees to raise silkworms and cultivating vineyards for the eventual production of wine. Both schemes were illegal, however, since both commodities would directly compete with Spain's silk and wine industries.

The government ordered the vineyards destroyed. Historian Fay Robinson portrays Hidalgo as a "quiet student [who] planted his vines in his leisure hours. In his lonely life they had been to him as children." She believes that what happened next moved Hidalgo to rebellion:

[Don Miguel] would not obey, and soldiers were sent to enforce the order. The fruits of his labor were destroyed; the vines were cut down and burned; but from their ashes arose a more maddening spirit than possibly even

Race and Class—Another View

In The Life and Times of Miguel Hidalgo y Costilla, *Arthur Howard Noll gives a description of race and class in Mexico, shedding light on the social situation of the country at the beginning of the nineteenth century.*

"There were the Old Spaniards, as they were at that time called, or white colonists of pure Spanish blood and of Spanish birth, comprising the only recognized society in the social organization that existed in Spanish America. It was apparently for them, and for the furtherance of their interests, that New Spain existed. For the latter part of the eighteenth century, especially since the accession of Carlos IV, they alone were permitted to fill the offices in the country; and so they might be found attached to the viceregal court, or occupying the offices of trust and profit, or engaged in whatever lucrative business might be pursued under the Spanish commercial system (which created monopolies, with all their attendant evils), or working the mines on a large scale. Hence they were chiefly gathered in the capital and in the larger towns of the provinces. They were wealthy, arrogant, and apt to be unscrupulous. They were firm supporters of Spain's unjust policy of government in America, both civil and ecclesiastical.

In the opposite social scale were the Indians, the pure native races who had scarcely been recognized as having any rights which the Old Spaniards were bound to respect. These were concentrated mainly in the vicinity of the large cities of the tableland.

A third class . . . was composed of creoles. These were regarded by the Old Spaniards in almost the same category as the native Indians.

There were besides these the mestizos, people of mixed Indian and Spanish blood, often confused with the creoles and possessing equal social rights with them; and a comparatively small number of mulattos, or mixed white and negroes; *zambos* or *Chinos*, Indians and negroes; and some African negroes, in the low lands adjacent to the Pacific coasts."

the vine had previously given birth to. This private wrong, added to the many oppressions to which he was subjected together with the mass of his countrymen, animated him.[10]

Don Miguel became more deeply involved in community activities. He joined the Querétaro Literary Club, one of many discussion groups in the region. Conversations often lasted for long hours, ranging far and wide over the political, social, and religious issues of the day. Creoles, and some *peninsulares* as well, were restless, and their discussion groups were a forum for planning change.

Discussion clubs were a natural arena for Don Miguel, whose wide-ranging reading (in Latin, Greek, Italian, and French as well as in Spanish) and zest for argument quickly made him a leading figure in the Querétaro group. The discussion groups were not literary societies or prayer meetings, but rather involved current events and social and economic analysis. "The idea of independence was being fostered throughout the Provincias by means of local clubs professedly of a social and literary character, in which, however, revolutionary plans were being freely discussed and sturdy patriotism was being inculcated,"[11] writes biographer Arthur Noll.

In addition to his participation at Querétaro, Don Miguel organized and hosted other discussion groups at his home. His discussion groups brought together all classes and races of people, including Indians, mestizos, and Creoles. Like those in Querétaro, Don Miguel's home discussion groups focused more and more on the need to move from words to action.

As the scorching, dusty summer of 1810 gave way to fall, the Querétaro Literary Club's discussions grew increasingly fiery. Revolution, not literature, was now the focus. December 8 was the date the conspirators chose for the beginning of the war for independence.

3 El Grito de Dolores

The members of the Querétaro Literary Club planned to begin their rebellion against colonial rule in early December 1810. Two members, rebellious Creole militia captains Ignacio Allende and Juan Aldama, planned to lead other militiamen members into battle against loyalist *peninsulares*. But others in the Querétaro Literary Club, though agreed on rebellion, saw a different scenario. Miguel Hidalgo's vision of revolution included mestizos and Indians, not just the elite Creoles and *peninsulares*. Before the revolutionaries could come to a final agreement among themselves, however, their plans were aborted.

Membership in the Querétaro club was wide open. Informers infiltrated the meetings, and a postal clerk betrayed the planned rebellion and its leaders to authorities. In early September, Doña Josefa Ortiz de Domínguez, a member of the club and the wife of a government official, learned that her husband had issued arrest warrants for Allende and Aldama. She sent a messenger to Dolores to warn of the betrayal.

When word of the betrayal and arrest orders reached them, Hidalgo, Allende, and Aldama could see but two alternatives: flight or an immediate call to arms that would include not just Creole soldiers

but all of the population. The Creoles, like Captains Allende and Aldama, would have been content with a shift in the balance of power, content to share power with their Spanish-born cousins. Most Creoles believed firmly in their own racial superiority as "pure-blooded" Europeans, though born in Mexico. Like the *peninsulares*, the Creole officers were an elite minority, accustomed to privilege. Not so the new, revolutionary army.

Ready to Fight

Hidalgo's troops came mostly from the Indians and mestizos of the countryside. Droughts in 1808, 1809, and 1810 had left them more poor and hungry than they had ever been. Thousands of unemployed and starving people had been forced to leave their homes and families, migrating to Mexico City to seek work and food. Too often they found no work and ended up begging on the streets. As described by historian Ramón Eduardo Ruiz, "The distribution of income grew more unequal. The rich were richer, and the poor were poorer. Widespread impoverishment, the handwork of listless wages and exploding inflation, partly explains the enthusiasm

Don Miguel as Organizer

From Bartolomé de Las Casas's defense of the Indians to twentieth-century liberation theologians and base Christian communities, one part of the church in the Americas has consistently advocated for the poorest, most oppressed of its people. Writing in The Life and Times of Miguel Hidalgo y Costilla, *Arthur Howard Noll describes how Don Miguel Hidalgo placed himself firmly in this company.*

"He was assured that the Indians had capacities for something better than slavery in the mines or on the haciendas, which had been imposed upon them by the *conquistadores* with their detestable system of *repartimientos* and *encomiendas*, and which had been continued to his time. His first thought was for their industrial education. He would develop their own industrial resources, and teach them how to value their freedom. These were remarkable plans to enter the mind of a creole ecclesiastic in New Spain in the early years of the nineteenth century. He would have been fifty years ahead of his time, had he been an Anglo-Saxon and held such ideas and formulated such plans. Being what he was, he was two centuries in advance of his age.

But Hidalgo's dreams were not alone of social and economic reforms: plans for political reform began to assume shape in his mind. Without political reforms, social and economic reforms were impossible. And from the prohibited books he read he had learned in what direction to look for the cause of the unhappiness of his people. . . .

It was due to bad government and to oppressive commercial laws emanating from the *Casa de Contratación* (another Spanish institution of the sixteenth century, which sought to control the trade of the dependencies for the sole benefit of the home government, and reduced to a minimum the industrial pursuits of the Spanish subjects in America, and the development of the rich resources of the country) that Mexico was so backward in civilization."

of the poor in the Bajío [southern Mexico] for the authors of Independence."[12]

Hidalgo found masses of Indians and mestizos ready to fight for independence and equality. His "troops" were not soldiers, however; no one could know whether they would fight bravely, how they would fare against professional soldiers, and whether they would respond to orders from their leaders.

The *peninsulares*, also called gachu-pínes, were natural targets of Hidalgo's followers. They represented the power of Spain, which had conquered the Indians of Mexico and had imposed laws that kept Indians and mestizos in the lowest place in society. Hidalgo's followers wanted to overturn the Spanish-run government.

Given the choice of giving up the revolution, or of relying on the relatively unknown army that Hidalgo could command, the three chose to call the people to their sides. A limited rebellion of one elite against another was no longer a possibility.

El Grito de Dolores

On September 16, 1810, Hidalgo rang the church bells, summoning the people of Dolores to mass. After the service, he

> addressed his congregation in words well calculated to incite them to insurrection. He drew a picture of the evils which rested over them; the iniquities of the Government to which they were subject and the advantages of independence. His venerable appearance, his voice and manner, and his attractive words aroused in them the greatest enthusiasm, and they gave a great shout, *"Viva Independencia! Viva America! Muere el mal gobierno!"* ("Long live Independence! Long live America! Death to bad government!") [13]

This rallying cry, delivered at the parish church of Dolores, is known as El Grito de Dolores. Such a call to action, or *grito*, was a traditional way to begin an important undertaking. Although at the time few people could read and write, many could remember and repeat the *grito*.

Indian rebellions against Spanish oppression had erupted throughout the two hundred years of occupation. Now, marching to battle under the banner of the Virgin of Guadalupe, the Indians had no intention of trading their Spanish-born rulers for Creole masters. "Death to gachupínes!" was a heartfelt vow, not mere rhetoric.

Masses of Indians and mestizos flocked to Hidalgo and the banner of the Virgin of Guadalupe. Within a few days, his army had grown to twenty thousand or more. Don Miguel was recognized as the head of the rebellion, and his title became Captain-General Hidalgo, and later Generalísimo Hidalgo. Captain Allende became Lieutenant General Allende.

Hidalgo and his army marched from Dolores to San Miguel el Grande. Only a few soldiers had firearms. What they lacked in firepower, however, they made up for in sheer numbers. Wielding machetes and slings, the revolutionaries easily captured San Miguel. But despite the efforts of Hidalgo and the few professional soldiers to keep order, the army soon turned into a mob. Rebel soldiers killed Spanish civilians as well as loyalist troops, stole their property, and burned their homes, all violations of traditional rules of warfare. After looting San Miguel, the revolutionary army marched on to Celaya, where the disorderly pillage continued.

Next in line was the provincial capital of Guanajuato, a town with a population of about seventy-five thousand. Much of Guanajuato's population seemed to be sympathetic to Hidalgo and his army. Not

Armed and ready to fight, Indian and mestizo revolutionaries join Hidalgo in his rebellion against Spanish oppression.

so the Spanish *intendente,* or provincial governor, Juan Antonio de Riaño, who prepared to resist. Expecting reinforcements, Riaño refused Hidalgo's request to surrender without a battle. The small contingent of Spaniards could not believe that they and their weapons could be beaten by a mob of Indians.

The *peninsulares* and soldiers barricaded themselves, their gold, and other valuables in the Alhóndiga, a structure normally used for storing merchandise. Most of the city's residents, however,

quickly pledged their allegiance to Hidalgo's cause. They had little in common with the Spaniards, and furthermore, they had been left outside the Alhóndiga without protection.

Hidalgo's army surrounded the Alhóndiga. From inside the building, Riaño gave the order to fire, and artillery and musket shots mowed down the attackers. Wave after wave of revolutionary soldiers surged toward the Alhóndiga, each new wave of men climbing over the bodies of the fallen. Eventually, Riaño was shot and killed by the revolutionaries. The defenders of the Alhóndiga, now leaderless, could not agree on a strategy. Historian Arthur Howard Noll describes what happened next:

Then occurred one of those deeds of bravery which are common in the annals of Mexican war, and which Mexican annalists love to recall. To bring the attack on the Alhóndiga to a speedy and satisfactory termination, Hidalgo called for a volunteer who would go under the walls and set fire to the large wooden doors which admitted to the patio. A young and sturdy worker in the mines came forward and, taking up a flat stone, tied it upon his back as a shield against missiles that might be thrown from the walls; then, with a torch in one hand, he crept on all fours to the door and set it on fire.[14]

As the doors fell, the mob surged in. Two thousand of their comrades had been killed by the Spaniards, and they were after revenge. Despite their leaders' attempts to stop them, Hidalgo's army killed everyone they could find inside the Alhóndiga. At least five hundred Spaniards died, and pillaging went on for nearly two days.

Fay Robinson, a nineteenth-century historian generally favorable to Hidalgo's cause, describes the pillage of Guanajuato:

The number of persons who fell in the defence and after it, is not known, and among them were many Mexican families connected by marriage with the obnoxious Spaniards. One family alone is said to have lost seventeen members; and the obstinate and prolonged defence could only have been made by a considerable number. We wish we could close our eyes to what followed;

This nineteenth-century painting portrays wealthy citizens of Guanajuato, one of the cities that Hidalgo's army pillaged in 1810.

but justice requires us to mention that *all* in the Alhóndega were slain. The Indians seemed to delight in repaying on their victims the grudges of three centuries; a matter of surprise to all, for they had lain so long dormant and submissive that it was supposed they had forgotten or become regardless of their former distinct nationality. This is not, however, astonishing, for the history of that people which has been enslaved and forgotten its lost freedom is yet to be written.[15]

Taking Guanajuato was both a practical and a symbolic victory of immense importance to the revolutionaries. The town's treasury yielded the equivalent of millions of dollars, funds that were much needed to sustain a revolutionary army. Individual rebels also gained by looting homes and businesses. The wealthier people of Guanajuato were their targets, whether Spanish or Creole or even mestizo. Hidalgo established a mint to produce coins, and a foundry to produce cannons and other arms for the revolution. Then he moved on.

Guanajuato was captured at the end of September 1810, barely two weeks after the beginning of the revolution. The

Education in Mexico

Spaniard Miguel Ramos de Arizpe recorded his findings about education in Mexico in the Report that Dr. Miguel Ramos de Arizpe, Priest of Borbon, and Deputy in the Present General and Special Cortes of Spain for the Province of Coahuila one of the Four Eastern Interior Provinces of the Kingdom of Mexico presents to the August Congress.

"The military posts and larger towns with donations from the garrisons and voluntary contributions of some parents support some inept persons of bad conduct who bear the title of teachers. These teachers as a rule waste their time in teaching the Christian doctrine badly, for they are usually incapable of imparting the fundamentals of a common public education. On the large estates where a large number of servants are used, it is customary to have one or more little schools. But more than once I have observed the care that has been taken to prevent the children of servants from learning to write, because some masters believe that if these children should learn to write, they would seek some other less unhappy way of living and would refuse the hard servitude in which their parents have lived. Unhappy American youth! Is it possible that their masters are trying to stunt the finest natural impulses and to keep man in brutal ignorance in order more easily to enslave him!"

progress of the revolution was extraordinarily rapid. From Guanajuato at the end of September, the revolutionaries marched to Zacatecas in early October, then to Valladolid by mid-October, and on to Monte de Las Cruces by October 30. Less than two months after its beginning in Dolores, the revolution arrived at the gates of Mexico City.

The Revolutionary Army on the March

The revolutionaries had grown in number from a few conspirators in a literary discussion club to an army variously estimated at fifty to eighty thousand. At times, the men of the army were joined by their wives and children. After the rebels took the provincial capital of Guanajuato, all of Mexico had to recognize them as a powerful force. The newest viceroy ordered troops to confront the rebels in battle. Hidalgo's army continued its march.

Even before El Grito de Dolores, a parish priest in Zacatecas, José María Cos, had warned of a growing hatred of Europeans. That hatred was directed at the city's small group of wealthy Spaniards. In early October, as the revolutionary army approached, the Spaniards of Zacatecas gathered their wealth and prepared to flee the city.

On October 7, the townspeople of Zacatecas seized control of the streets and prevented the Spaniards from leaving. Mineworkers demanded immediate payment of overdue wages. In this atmosphere of fear and turmoil, the Spanish *intendente*, Francisco Rendón, gave up control of the town to Mexican-born Conde de Santiago de la Laguna. Laguna, whose sympathies were with the revolution, nevertheless took command of the government troops. He used them to safeguard the Spanish flight from Zacatecas, preventing a massacre. Hidalgo then named Laguna *intendente* of Zacatecas and an officer in the revolutionary army, but months later, Laguna was removed from office and arrested because he continued to safeguard the Spanish elites and protect their property.

Sympathy for the revolutionary cause also ran high in San Luis Potosí, where local priests and military officials conspired to take control of the city. They handed it over to the revolutionary forces in mid-November.

The march of revolution had reached Valladolid in mid-October. There Hidalgo proclaimed in large measure the revolutionary platform. He decreed an end to slavery and an end to forced payment of tribute by Indians to the Spanish. Hidalgo denounced the system of *castas*, which classified people by race and social status at birth. Hidalgo's sympathies were clearly with the poor, and theirs with the charismatic priest. His army and his power did not come from the Creoles of his own class. The revolution came from the vast, disenfranchised majority of Indians and mestizos. In addition, approximately four hundred priests joined Hidalgo; they represented the interests of the lower clergy against the wealthy hierarchy of the church.

That hierarchy acted to protect the interests of the wealthy *peninsulares*, and its own control of the church and its property, by excommunicating Hidalgo. Excommunication is an official condemnation of an individual by the church. It amounts to cutting that individual off from all the rites and benefits of the church and proclaiming that his or her soul will go to hell. The bishop of Valladolid proclaimed the excommunication of Hidalgo, and it was confirmed by the Inquisition. Anyone who questioned its validity was also ordered excommunicated.

Although the bishop of Valladolid opposed Hidalgo, the people of Valladolid welcomed him. He and his army were joined by many of Valladolid's militia and trained soldiers, and by Don José María Morelos, a priest and an old friend. Morelos would become an important revolutionary leader in his own right. As church and government authorities had fled before his arrival, Hidalgo seized their abandoned treasury. Then, on October 19, Hidalgo and his army marched out of Valladolid toward Mexico City.

Mestizo priest Don José María Morelos joined Hidalgo's revolutionary march in Valladolid.

The Tide of Battle Turns

On October 30, about sixty thousand troops under the joint command of Hidalgo and Allende met a Mexican army force of about seven thousand commanded by a Colonel Trujillo. They joined in battle in the mountain pass of Monte de Las Cruces. The revolutionaries defeated the vastly outnumbered regular army, as might be expected, but the cost of victory was high to an army lacking in equipment, arms, and discipline.

At one point in the battle, a revolutionary officer approached the regular army lines under a flag of truce. Under the rules of war, the flag-bearing officer should have been immune from attack. Instead, the regular army commander, Colonel Trujillo, ordered him killed, a shocking violation in an era in which armies observed codes of conduct in warfare as a matter of honor.

Colonel Trujillo boasted of his act, saying that the rules of war need not be

Cities Captured by Hidalgo's Army

Hidalgo's Rebellion, 1810–1811

observed against the revolutionaries. In effect, the Spanish still could not regard their Indian, mestizo, and Creole opponents as a "real" army. Even though the revolutionary leaders had been unable to stop their untrained, undisciplined army from looting and pillaging, they were angered by this blatant show of disrespect.

Now Hidalgo's army stood virtually at the gates of Mexico City. Victory seemed at hand. The Spanish viceroy, with little hope of successfully defending the city, ordered a statue of the Virgin de los Remedios brought to the cathedral. He laid his baton of office before the statue of the Virgin, declaring her the general of the Spanish army. Both sides were ready for battle, each under the banner of its own Virgin.

From a military standpoint, it seemed that nothing could stop the march of the revolutionaries. Allende stood ready to lead them to complete victory. No army stood between them and the capital. But Hidalgo then made a shocking move. He

ordered a retreat. While historians can only guess at his reasoning, most believe that Hidalgo feared what his army would do to Mexico City. He may have wanted to avoid the potential massacre of its Spanish residents. Less than two months into the revolution, Hidalgo had seen too much looting, too much bloodshed. He would not allow more of it in his country's capital.

Turning back from Mexico City proved to be a strategic error on a grand scale. On November 17, the retreating revolutionaries met the army of General Felix Calleja del Rey at San Geronimo de Aculco. In the bloody and ferocious battle that followed, the revolutionary army was badly defeated. Hidalgo himself barely escaped to continue his retreat. General Calleja boasted that Hidalgo lost ten thousand men in this battle. While most historians emphasize the savagery of Hidalgo's Indian troops, few accounts note that "of these [ten thousand], five thousand had been put to the sword in total disregard of the rules of war."[16]

Calleja pursued the retreating army, defeating Allende and then recapturing Guanajuato. There Calleja massacred all of the inhabitants to punish them for supporting the revolution. Fourteen thousand men, women, and children were rounded up in the town square and butchered by Calleja's troops.

In retaliation for Calleja's massacre, Hidalgo ordered the execution of forty-one Spaniards in Valladolid. The Spaniards were captured enemies, prisoners of war. The executions, and the earlier killing of Spanish civilians and looting of homes in conquered towns by Hidalgo's army, were, again, clear violations of the rules of war. Noll calls the executions "the act of a man who was not in his nature blood-thirsty, but was wrought up to a high nervous condition by the scenes through which he was

General Felix Calleja del Rey led his troops to a series of victories against Hidalgo's army, temporarily quelling the tide of the revolution.

passing and by a contemplation of the acts of savage cruelty of his enemies."[17]

Despite Calleja's string of victories, Hidalgo still had considerable support in many areas. He made a triumphant entrance into Guadalajara on November 26. Allende joined him on December 12. In Guadalajara, Hidalgo tried to organize a government, appointing ministers and an ambassador to the United States.

At the beginning of 1811, Hidalgo still commanded an army estimated at eighty thousand. He had lost thirty thousand during the battles of the preceding months. Under various generals, the revolutionaries held a wide swath of territory, including the towns of Guadalajara, Saltillo, Aguascalientes, and Zacatecas. Hidalgo had begun publication of *El despertador americano* (*The American Alarmist*), a periodical that published his platform for change.

In addition to the military contest between the revolutionary army and the government soldiers, Hidalgo was under renewed investigation by the Holy Office. By law, church authorities had complete jurisdiction over him because he was a priest. Neither civil nor military courts could legally put a priest on trial, so the Holy Office investigation was a significant procedure.

Defeat for Hidalgo

In January, General Calleja appeared at Guadalajara, ready to drive Hidalgo's forces out. His seven thousand well-armed, well-disciplined soldiers took only two days to rout the poorly armed revolutionary army. Hidalgo and Allende escaped, and refused the pardon offered

The Other Revolutions

The 1775 revolution of the thirteen American colonies and the 1789 French Revolution were both significant to educated Mexicans. Some, like Hidalgo and his friends, found inspiration in them. Others, more conservative and less inclined to change, thought these revolutions were appalling. Jasper Ridley describes some of the reactions to revolution in Maximilian and Juárez.

"Then, . . . in Philadelphia, they had adopted Thomas Jefferson's Declaration of Independence, with its absurd and blasphemous statement that 'all men are created equal.' Was it not plain that God had created men unequal, some to be princes and some to be subjects, some to be lords and some to be serfs, some to be rich and some to be poor, some to be masters and some to be slaves? And the Americans themselves were hypocrites when they professed to believe that all men were equal, because they owned black slaves and had exterminated the Indians. . . .

What most distressed the conservatives about the American Revolution was the part that Spain, their beloved Spain, had played in bringing it about. . . . [T]he Spanish pride of the Mexican conservatives led them to exaggerate the role of Spain, and their guilty consciences made them blame the folly of the well-intentioned but misguided King Charles III, who in order to regain Florida from the British had encouraged the idea of revolution throughout the whole American hemisphere.

The French Revolution had an even more serious effect on Mexico. The revolutionaries in Paris proclaimed the doctrine of liberty, equality, and fraternity, and the rights of man, which Pope Pius VI anathematized as evil and heretical, for man had no rights, only the duty to serve God in the station in society in which the Almighty had placed him by obeying his superiors, showing kindness to his inferiors, and believing and upholding the doctrines of the Catholic Church."

them if they would renounce their cause. Pardon, they replied, was for criminals, not for patriots.

After the defeat, the revolutionary leaders agreed that Hidalgo must resign his position as general of the armies. He immediately acquiesced, becoming solely a political leader. Allende became the new general. A lawyer, Ignacio Aldama, was sent as minister plenipotentiary, a kind of special ambassador, to seek the aid of the United States. He was captured and executed by government military forces.

Hidalgo and Allende, with other leaders, set out for New Orleans also intending to petition the United States for support. They never made it to New Orleans.

Ignacio Elizondo, a colonel in the viceroy's army, had defected to the side of the revolution. Now Elizondo changed sides again and betrayed Hidalgo and Allende. On March 21, 1811, all the revolutionary leaders were taken prisoner in the desert and moved to Monclova. Then, in chains day and night, they were taken hundreds of miles farther, to Chihuahua.

At Chihuahua, the military leaders of the revolution were tried for treason before a military court, convicted, and shot.

Though his efforts did not gain independence for Mexico, Hidalgo's dream did not end with his death. Several other leaders stood poised to take up the cause.

As a priest, however, Hidalgo needed to be condemned by the church, not by a civil or military court. The military authorities lost patience waiting for the case to make its way through the church bureaucracy: They found a bishop who declared Hidalgo no longer a priest, tried him for treason, and executed him on July 30, 1811. The heads of Hidalgo, Allende, and Aldama were brought to Guanajuato and displayed on pikes at the Alhóndiga until 1825.

With the heads of the leaders cut off, many thought that the revolution was forever at an end. And so it might have been had the movement rested in man's hand—that is, had it originated solely with those men, or with any one set of men, or had it been dependent for its final success on aught else than the mighty power of progress. Independence was not an accident. It had waited its full development in the womb of time, and now its bringing-forth was certain. The birth of freedom in America had long been predetermined. Cut off the head of every revolutionist twenty times, and

Ignacio de Allende, one of the original leaders of the Mexican War of Independence, was executed for his role in the revolution.

twenty times new armies would arise until the great dragon was slain.[18]

The revolution, though beheaded, was alive. By the time Hidalgo, Allende, and Aldama died, their cause had been taken up by other leaders around the country.

4 Morelos and Iturbide Inherit the Revolution

Just as Allende and Hidalgo differed in their aims and beliefs, so did the leaders who followed them. One group, wealthier and better educated, planned to win Mexican independence but wanted no changes in the basic structure of the government and economy. These men, called *criollos letrados*, or educated Creoles, believed that Creoles should take the place of the *peninsulares*, becoming the new ruling class of Mexico. Hidalgo's vision of equality for all was carried on by another priest, José María Morelos y Pavón, who inherited Hidalgo's popular and military leadership roles.

Ignacio López Rayón, the leader of the *criollos letrados*, was a well-educated Creole lawyer. He had served as Hidalgo's personal secretary, and had also organized troops in the northern part of Mexico. After the deaths of Allende and Hidalgo, López Rayón moved south, joining other Creole rebels in Michoacán.

Morelos, a short, dark-skinned, chubby man, was born in a Michoacán village, the son of a carpenter. His mother was the daughter of a schoolteacher. His ancestors included Africans as well as Indians and Spaniards.

After working as a mule driver in his youth, Morelos became a priest at the age of thirty. He studied for a time at the Cole-gio San Nicolás, where Miguel Hidalgo taught, and came to respect and admire the older man.

When the revolution began, Morelos was the mestizo pastor of an impoverished parish in Michoacán. He immediately sought out his old teacher. Hidalgo was

After Hidalgo's death, Morelos (pictured) used his military genius to carry out Hidalgo's quest for equality and independence.

then the military as well as the popular leader of the revolution. After long discussion of the religious justification for revolution, Hidalgo commissioned Morelos as a military officer in the army of the revolution. He sent Morelos off to wage war in southern Mexico. As might be expected, Morelos championed the cause of the Indians and mestizos and African slaves.

Morelos and Guerrilla Warfare

The southern jungles and "hot country" between the Pacific Coast and the central plateaus were familiar territory to Morelos. In addition, he proved a natural leader and soldier. At first, Morelos employed European military tactics and organization. He organized his soldiers in units, taught them to march in unison, and led them out to meet the opposing army head-on in battle. Morelos's troops were recruited from peasants and laborers and had at most a few weeks of training. Their weapons were often machetes or swords, not the guns that equipped the government's army. Thus, the traditional style of warfare gave a great advantage to the well-trained, well-armed military forces of the government.

Morelos soon resorted to a new style of fighting better suited to his army—guerrilla warfare. In guerrilla warfare, flexible groups of fighters engage in harassment, sabotage, and quick attacks, and then fade away into the countryside. By using guerrilla tactics, Morelos's soldiers could take advantage of their superior knowledge of the territory, as well as their popular support. Small groups of fighters could rely on the people of the countryside to hide them, feed them, and warn them of the government army's approach.

Morelos recruited blacks, mulattos, Indians, and mestizos. His soldiers substituted their familiar machetes for swords. Despite their lack of military training and armament, Morelos and his soldiers were a formidable match for the government armies.

From the beginning, Morelos clearly communicated his beliefs. Skin color and social class, he preached, did not determine a person's worth. The land should belong to those who farmed it. All the children of the land, not just the wealthy, deserved good schools. He believed fervently in the Virgin of Guadalupe and the Roman Catholic Church. He also praised the heroism of the Indian chiefs who fought against Cortés to keep their freedom.

Morelos had joined the revolution in October 1810, just a month after it began. By January of the following year, while Hidalgo's army was in virtual retreat, pursued by General Calleja, Morelos and his army had taken the important city of Acapulco. Morelos's army was smaller and better disciplined than the hordes who followed Hidalgo. In capturing Acapulco, it took seven hundred prisoners and treated them, as in other cities, humanely. Morelos's victory over a better-armed royalist force brought him fame and new recruits from around the country.

Throughout 1811, until Hidalgo and the other military leaders of the revolution were captured and executed in the north, Morelos and his army consolidated their control in the south. Late in 1811, after the executions of Hidalgo and Allende, the *criollos letrados* formed a junta, or governing board, in the southern city of Zitácuaro. The junta of Zitácuaro included López Rayón, José Liceaga, José Sixto Verdugo, Carlos Maria de Bustamante, Andrés Quintana Roo, and José María Cos. López Rayón presided over the junta, which named Morelos as its military commander in chief.

José Morelos

José Morelos, like Hidalgo, was a priest. Unlike Hidalgo, he proved to be a brilliant military tactician. In Mexico, Past and Present, *G. B. Winton calls him an Indian. In* Maximilian and Juárez, *Jasper Ridley says he is a mestizo. Here, the two historians differ in their accounts of the same persons and events.*

"A little dark-faced Indian, [writes Winton] who had obtained his theological training after years of manual labor and poverty, partly under Hidalgo while the great patriot was rector of the Colegio de San Nicolás, Morelos, when his old teacher came back to Valladolid at the head of an army, was curate of a near-by village. When he hastened to join the revolutionary movement, which exactly suited his tastes, Hidalgo, instead of taking him along on his march toward the capital, sent him flying southward with orders to gather troops and, if possible, take possession of Acapulco, a port on the Pacific coast. Sallying forth alone and without resources, the martial priest so successfully carried out the orders of his superior as to enroll his name among the really great military leaders of the world. His exploits, if detailed, would make a romance as thrilling as any ever born in the imagination of genius."

"The revolutionary struggle [writes Ridley] was carried on by another priest, a mestizo named José Morelos. Unlike Hidalgo, he organized the rebels into a disciplined force, forbade looting, and spared the lives of his prisoners. That made no impression on General Calleja, who systematically executed every rebel he captured. It was only in the closing months of the revolt, after all his protests to Calleja had failed, that Morelos ordered reprisals, executing prisoners and burning the property of government supporters. The rebellion was suppressed and Morelos was shot in December 1815, after he had been degraded from the priesthood and excommunicated as a heretic. One of the charges brought against him by the Inquisition was that he had a portrait of Hidalgo in his possession."

Now General Calleja marched south, intent on first destroying the junta and then defeating Morelos. The junta was their top priority since the *peninsulares* in Mexico City saw a greater threat in Creole politicians than in a mestizo priest-general.

Morelos had military ability and the power conferred by his followers. Unfortunately for him, Morelos seemed to agree that the Creole politicians were key to the revolution. Despite his own strong beliefs, he allied himself with the Creole junta. Perhaps Morelos was intimidated, despite his belief in equality, by the Creoles' superior education and their air of command. Or perhaps he was driven to an alliance by the approach of Calleja, who was heading south to capture or destroy the junta, believing that "the enemy of my enemy must be my friend."

Historians differ in their judgments of Morelos. Some feel he made the logical choice in accepting the leadership of people who were smarter than he was. Others believe that he betrayed his followers and his ideals by joining forces with the junta.

General Calleja reached Zitácuaro on New Year's Day 1812 to find the junta had escaped. His army nevertheless razed Zitácuaro's walls, burned its houses, and indiscriminately killed residents. On January 14, Calleja marched out to take on Morelos and his army, who were encamped not far away at Cuautla Amilpas. General Calleja and his Spanish and Creole officers did not think highly of Morelos and his army. The revolutionaries, however, proved more than a match for Calleja, defeating his forces in a ferocious eight-hour battle on January 19. A contemporary historian describes the scene that day:

On this occasion Morelos had the satisfaction to see his negro levies meet the Spanish veterans with a firmness which realized all he had hoped, but dared not anticipate. On the 19th, Calleja assaulted the town in four columns, with great fierceness. The Mexicans suffered him to approach till within one hundred yards, when they opened on them a fire which could not be withstood. The Spaniards fled precipitately, and Galeaño [a revolutionary fighter], having discovered a Spanish colonel seeking to rally his men, sallied out, and in a hand-to-hand contest killed him. The consequence was that all four columns were repulsed, after an action which lasted from seven A.M. till three P.M., and Calleja was forced to retreat, having lost five hundred men.[19]

The battle once again proved the courage and military ability of Morelos's revolutionary troops. Fighting ability, however, was not enough. While Morelos protected the junta, he could not govern it. López Rayón and his fellow Creoles argued endlessly among themselves and were unable to agree on their goals and plans for government.

Congress of Chilpancingo

Finally, in September 1813, Morelos called a congress in Chilpancingo, in the southern state of Guerrero, to write a constitution. The congress was both larger and more representative than the junta, including Creole leaders of the revolution and representatives from various provinces of Mexico.

Morelos presented the mostly Creole congress with a declaration called "Sentiments of the Nation." According to historian Jan Bazant, this document proposed that

America [Mexico] should be free and independent of Spain and any other nation, government, or monarchy. The Catholic religion should be the only religion, without the toleration of any other; its ministers should be supported by the tithes and the first fruits only and the dogma should be upheld by the hierarchy consisting of Pope, bishops, and curates, "for every plant which God did not plant should be torn out," probably a reference to the unpopular inquisition. Morelos made it clear that the form of government should be republican. Slavery, tribute, and all ethnic distinctions were to be abolished and all Mexicans—called "Americans"—would be equal. Their property should be respected and laws should regulate poverty and destitution and increase the wages of the poor.[20]

Before acting on the constitution, the Creoles of the congress debated political philosophy with one another for more than a month. Meanwhile, according to one account, they ate up all the town's food and used what amounted to tons of paper. Finally, in November 1813, they declared Mexico's independence from Spain.

As the congress continued to debate specifics for an independent Mexico, Morelos continued his military campaign. His army was driven from Cuautla by government forces, but then briefly conquered Orizaba. Driven from Orizaba, he took the entire province of Oaxaca. There Morelos released all political prisoners from the jails, and freed some common prisoners as well.

After a victorious march, Morelos and his rebel army laid siege to Mexico City itself. Now their fortunes turned. General Calleja broke the rebel siege, freeing Mexico City from any immediate threat of rebel conquest. The general then marched on Chilpancingo, where the Creole congress was still assembled. Morelos's army got there first and escorted the congress out of Chilpancingo to refuge in Apatzingán. There the congress promulgated the Constitution of Chilpancingo, also known as the *Decreto de Apatzingán.*

The constitution endorsed universal male suffrage, popular sovereignty, and Catholicism as the official religion. It abolished slavery, the *castas* system, government monopolies, and torture of convicted criminals. It emphasized "economic liberty" and private property. Yet it spoke not one word about the agrarian reform called for by both Hidalgo and Morelos.

In 1815, Morelos was captured and executed by government troops. His death was a blow to the revolution and an occasion of great sorrow for revolutionaries, especially for the poor whose cause he had championed. Because the congress and the Creole politicians had been dependent on Morelos and his army for protection, some people thought (and some hoped) that his death would end the war for independence. That did not happen. Although the revolutionary armies were scattered, guerrilla fighting continued in scattered actions. Despite the apparent victory of the colonial government, the desire of Mexicans for self-rule had not been extinguished.

From Waging War to Making a Government

While the criollos letrados *may have taken the lead in writing down and formalizing a new plan of government, Morelos supported this move, according to William Davis Robinson in* Memoirs of the Mexican Revolution.

"Morelos, in the midst of his military successes, appeared more anxious for the welfare of his country, than to display the character of a military chieftain. He was the first to propose and promote the formation of a civil government, and thereby gave an unequivocal proof of his patriotism. He frequently acknowledged, to his intimate friends, that he wished to divide a responsibility, which he felt himself unequal to sustain. With these views, he convened a congress. It was composed of forty members, from the different provinces. Don José María Liceaga was elected president. A constitution was framed, at Apatzinjan in the province of Valladolid, accepted, and sworn to, throughout all the provinces which had taken up arms in favour of the republic. Whatever may be the defects of that constitution, it certainly displays more wisdom, than could have been expected from men, brought up as the framers of it had been, and situated as they were."

One colonial military officer, a Creole who felt that his talents were insufficiently recognized and rewarded by the colonial government, eventually led Mexico to independence from Spain. His name was Agustín de Iturbide.

Agustín de Iturbide came from a Spanish noble family, but was himself born in Mexico on September 27, 1783, the eldest of five children. His father served as a municipal officer in the city of Valladolid, now called Morelia.

By the time Iturbide was fifteen years old, he not only managed one of his father's haciendas but had also been commissioned as a second lieutenant in the eight-hundred-man Valladolid infantry regiment. The regiment probably contained only a few professional, year-round soldiers, with most of its members, like Iturbide, spending only a month as a soldier each year. In 1805, Iturbide married Ana María Huarte, the wealthy and beautiful daughter of the provincial *intendente*. After his marriage, Iturbide appears to have served on active duty in his regiment. He was sent to Mexico City and then to Jalapa for military training.

The contest for power between the *peninsulares* of the ruling *audiencias* and the Creole elites forced military officers to choose sides. Lieutenant Iturbide followed the lead of another military officer, Felix Calleja, and placed himself on the side of *peninsulares* like his father.

Iturbide: Loyalist Officer

Iturbide was utterly unsympathetic to the revolution begun by Hidalgo and his allies. He described his own reaction:

When the insurrection began, I was at the hacienda of Apeo on an indefinite furlough from military service which had been granted to me by Señor Lizanza in order that I might recover from a serious illness from which I was suffering. On September 20 I received news of the outbreak of the rebellion. At once I planned to proceed to the capital city. Upon arriving there, I presented myself to his Excellency Señor Venegas. I made known to him my desire to engage actively in the royal ser-

---

Guadalupe Victoria

The war that continued after the defeat and death of Morelos was a true guerrilla war. Guadalupe Victoria was one of the leaders who kept the flame of revolution alive. William Davis Robinson describes Guadalupe Victoria in Memoirs of the Mexican Revolution.

"Don Guadalupe Victoria at no time had under his command more than two thousand men; but he was so well-acquainted with the fastnesses of the province of Vera Cruz that the royalists never could bring him to a general action. In vain, they sent superior forces to attack him; in vain they drove him from one position to another; for, as fast as they destroyed part of his forces in one place, he recruited them to another. More than twenty times, the Mexican *Gazette* has published that Victoria was slain, and his party annihilated; but, a few days after those false and pompous accounts, we have heard of Victoria suddenly springing up, attacking and capturing convoys of merchandise, seizing some strongholds, and throwing the whole country into consternation. At the head of one hundred and fifty or two hundred cavalry, he performed some of the most daring exploits that were effected during the revolution; and his personal courage and activity were universally acknowledged, even by his enemies. Wherever he went, provisions were secretly or openly furnished him. Had he possessed muskets, there were from ten to fifteen thousand men ready to accept them, and join his standard. To the want of arms and munitions of war, and to no other cause, must be attributed his final failure."

---

vice. Honorable, talented, and influential persons gave him good reports about me.[21]

When the rebels conquered Valladolid, Iturbide's family fled from their home. The insurgents sacked the homes and businesses of many wealthy Spaniards and Creoles. The hacienda of the Iturbide family was among them. According to Iturbide, Hidalgo offered to pardon his father and to protect the whole family if only Agustín Iturbide would change sides. Iturbide refused the offer.

Iturbide's military exploits continued after Hidalgo's death. In 1813, General Calleja, ruthless pursuer of rebels, was named viceroy. In his turn, Iturbide was appointed colonel of a new regiment and commander of the Spanish army in Guanajuato. He continued in pursuit of both Morelos and fame. At about this time, Iturbide applied for a high military honor, the Order of San Fernando, basing his application on his military exploits and loyalty. He was upset when his application was denied.

Conveniently forgetting a few failures, Iturbide boasted that he fought wherever sent and won every battle, even when the enemy outnumbered his troops by more than ten to one. His superiors agreed that he was a first-rate military officer. He was named commander of the Army of the North, as well as of Guanajuato and Valladolid. Still, Iturbide felt that he had not received the recognition due a military leader of his talents. He also knew that, as a Creole officer, he faced little hope of advancement in government.

As a commanding officer, Iturbide showed both military ability and ruthlessness:

Agustín de Iturbide, a colonial military officer, wanted to win Mexico's independence from Spain, but he also wanted to preserve the wealth and power of the privileged classes.

From the hacienda of Villachuato, Iturbide issued an order which became notorious in Mexican military annals. He announced that to prevent the spread of the rebellious spirit he had decided to separate the insurgents in his district from its loyal inhabitants. In an arbitrary fashion he directed that, after the lapse of three days, the followers, the wives, and the children of malcontents of whatever stripe were to be meted out the same harsh treatment as that accorded to rebel soldiers bearing arms. Asserting that he respected both the merit and the important service of Iturbide, on January 6, 1815, the curate Antonio de Labarrieta sent a protest to the Viceroy against the inhumanity of an order which menaced women and children with imprisonment. Labarrieta maintained that Spanish piety and generosity would not sanction such a horrible policy. "Holy God," he exclaimed, "what times have come upon us!"[22]

Iturbide next proposed to Calleja that he would execute one-tenth of the imprisoned wives of the guerrillas. If a Spanish soldier were murdered, Iturbide said, then all of the wives would be executed. If resistance continued in any way, he would raze towns that had been rebel territory. Viceroy Calleja vetoed these proposals.

Complaints Against Iturbide

In 1816, Iturbide was relieved of his command and recalled to Mexico City. Complaints about his greed and cruelty in administering the territory that he had conquered had reached the viceroy. Iturbide's critics pointed out that he had become very wealthy during his time as a military commander, far more wealthy than was possible on his military salary.

The strongest criticism of Iturbide came from Antonio de Labarrieta, the priest who had protested Iturbide's 1815 order. Labarrieta accused Iturbide of unjustly imprisoning both men and women, whether or not they were proven guilty of rebellion or crime. He further charged that Iturbide had illegally enriched himself, and had damaged agriculture, trade, and mining in the Bajío territories under his command.

Iturbide vehemently denied all charges made against him. Initial investigations found many people in Guanajuato reluctant to speak for fear that Iturbide would be restored to power there. Friends and allies came quickly to his defense.

The viceroy himself investigated, listened to Iturbide's friends, and investigated further. In a letter to the Spanish minister of war, Viceroy Calleja complained that he frequently found that "an officer, who by his valor and intelligence is fitted to command a division in a campaign, often lacks the talent required for civil and political administration or engages in his former mercantile occupation."[23] In the end, no charges were brought against Iturbide, but he was not restored to his command of the Bajío.

The experience undoubtedly heightened Iturbide's resentment of the *peninsular* government. He remained in Mexico City, spending lavishly and squandering the fortune that he had accumulated. Back in the Bajío, Iturbide's military successors proved unable to stop raids by one of Morelos's successors, Vicente Guerrero, and his bands of guerrillas. Together with an Indian leader, Pedro Asencio, Guerrero had continued to fight long after Morelos's death. In 1820, Viceroy Calleja sent Iturbide back to the Bajío to offer the

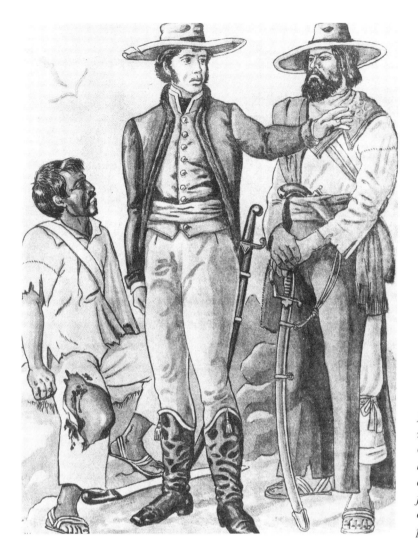

Iturbide met resistance from rebel leader Vicente Guerrero. Guerrero, shown here flanked by guerrilla fighters, was one of the rebels who continued fighting in Morelos's honor and refused Iturbide's offer of peace.

guerrillas a choice between peace and death.

The peace offer was in the form of a pardon, offered by Spain to all rebels in 1820. In that year, King Ferdinand VII of Spain accepted the Spanish Constitution of 1812. As part of the new order of constitutional government, the king sought reconciliation with insurgents throughout Spain's colonies. In addition, delegates from the colonies were to be sent to Spain as members of the Spanish Cortes, or congress.

The Spanish Constitution of 1812 was the product of European wars, not of the Mexican War of Independence. It set forth rules for how Spain was to be governed, not Mexico. And the delegates to be sent from the colonies were not to be rebels, but rather delegates to be selected by colonial governments. Dissatisfied, the Mexican rebels refused the pardon and peace offer.

Although the guerrillas rejected the pardon proposal, Iturbide pursued them with little enthusiasm. Government authorities had listened to his critics, and had not given him the honors he thought he deserved. Iturbide now saw his future as an officer in the Mexican army was limited.

While writing to the viceroy about his plans to exterminate the rebels, Iturbide was also writing to friends about a different plan. He sent drafts of a plan for independence and a new Mexican government to his allies in the church and military, asking some to edit and polish it. At least some of the thirty Mexican delegates to the Spanish congress knew about the plan. Some met secretly with Iturbide. Some advocated delay before unveiling the plan and forming a Mexican congress. Others were dubious about Iturbide's leadership. Without reaching a final decision, all of the delegates sailed for Spain in early February 1821.

The Plan of Iguala

Shortly after the delegates left for Spain, Iturbide assembled his officers at Iguala. On February 24, 1821, he unveiled his plan, the Plan of Iguala, which called for Mexican independence. Three of its provisions became key rallying points:

1. That Mexico should form an independent empire, the crown of which should be offered to the king of Spain, and, in the event of his refusal, to the other princes of his family in succession, on condition that the person accepting should reside in the country, and should swear to observe a constitution to be fixed by a congress;

2. That the Roman Catholic religion should be supported, and the rights, immunities, and property of its clergy should be preserved and secured;

3. That all the actual inhabitants of Mexico, whatever might be their birthplace or descent, should enjoy the same civil rights.[24]

These three points became known as the "Three Guarantees."

Iturbide had apparently had a change of heart. No longer was he a defender of Spain and the *peninsular* government. And even though Iturbide had been the enemy of revolution, the revolutionaries were now ready to accept him as a leader. Vicente Guerrero and Pedro Asencio joined forces with Iturbide and his soldiers in the so-called Army of the Three Guarantees. They swore to uphold independence for Mexico, the Catholic religion, and union between European-born and Mexican-born residents.

Iturbide's Plan of Iguala, which ran to more than twenty separate articles, had broad appeal. One provision called for King Ferdinand VII to live in Mexico and reign there. Although there was no reason to believe that the king had any desire to live in Mexico as its monarch, this article reassured people loyal to the king and to the idea of monarchy.

The Plan of Iguala did not contain the revolutionary measures advocated by Hidalgo, but it did appeal to his followers by legally abolishing distinctions of race and caste. Prosperous Creoles liked the plan for two reasons: First, it was written by one of their own, a land-owning, Creole military chieftain. Second, it abolished special privileges for Europeans.

Iturbide's Army of the Three Guarantees in a procession through Mexico City in 1821. The Three Guarantees promised Mexican independence, allegiance to the Catholic Church, and equality for all.

The church had suffered the elimination of many clerical privileges under the Spanish Constitution of 1812. The plan's enthusiastic endorsement of religion was reassuring to church leaders. In short, Iturbide's Plan of Iguala had something for every Mexican.

Iturbide: Revolutionary Leader

With many officers and soldiers coming to his side, Iturbide launched a two-pronged campaign of military strategy and propaganda. He called for all soldiers and all Mexicans to join his side. And he marched out to conquer towns that did not do so voluntarily. Some towns, like Guanajuato, surrendered without bloodshed. Others were overcome by Iturbide's superior force.

The contrast with Iturbide's conduct as a royalist officer pursuing rebels could not have been greater. As the loyal government officer, he had killed or imprisoned rebels and threatened their families with death. Now, as he led his own army of rebellion, Iturbide treated even conquered

Guerrilla leader Nicolás Bravo was one of many rebels who eventually pledged their loyalty to Iturbide.

cities and soldiers graciously. Surrendering royalist troops were given back their swords and knapsacks and allowed to choose where they wished to live.

Rebel as well as royalist troops joined Iturbide's march. Guadalupe Victoria, another Morelos follower, emerged from the mountains of Veracruz. And guerrilla leader Nicolás Bravo, freed from a dungeon by the viceroy in early 1821, received the rank of colonel in Iturbide's army.

In July, soldiers in Mexico City rose in support of Iturbide and captured Viceroy Juan de Apodaca, who had been appointed to replace Viceroy Calleja in 1816. He agreed to resign in return for safe passage to the port city of Veracruz for himself and his family. With the viceroy's resignation, Spain's official representative in Mexico was now a military officer, Captain-General Juan O'Donojú.

In August, Iturbide met O'Donojú at Veracruz. O'Donojú had few choices. He did not have the resources to oppose Iturbide by military means. If he opposed Iturbide, his defeat would seem to be Spain's defeat.

Though not authorized to do so by the Spanish king, O'Donojú signed a treaty recognizing Mexican independence on August 24, 1821. He rationalized that at least the new plan recognized the king and gave O'Donojú, as Spain's representative, a voice in government. He wrote to Spain to explain why he found it necessary to recognize Mexican independence and Iturbide's power:

> All the provinces of New Spain had proclaimed their independence. Either by force or by virtue of capitulations, all the strongholds had opened their gates to the champions of liberty. They had a force of 30,000 soldiers of all arms, organized and disciplined. . . . This army was directed by men of talent and character. At the head of these forces there was a commander who knew how to inspire them and how to secure their favor and their love. This commander had always led them to victory. He had on his side all the prestige that is usually bestowed upon heroes.[25]

In just six months, Iturbide had won independence for Mexico.

The treaty signed by Iturbide and O'Donojú provided for a provisional junta to govern Mexico until a permanent government was established. O'Donojú was to be a member of that junta. The junta would assemble a congress, choose a president of that body, and appoint three persons to serve as the executive while awaiting the arrival of a Spanish prince to assume the title of emperor of Mexico. If no royal were to accept, the Mexican congress could choose an emperor.

By the end of September, Iturbide and O'Donojú were in full possession of Mexico City. Iturbide was greeted as a liberator. The junta appointed by Iturbide included upper-class Mexicans, but none of the early rebels who had spent more than ten years fighting for their revolution. The thirty-eight-member junta named five regents to govern the country. Iturbide was named both president of the regency and military commander in chief.

The first elected Mexican congress was convened in February 1822. Most members were rich Creoles (*letrados*) and lawyers. Factions quickly became apparent. One group, loyal to the king if not to Spain, was known as the Bourbon faction, after the name of the Spanish royal line. A second, loyal to Iturbide, the "Generalissimo de Tierra y Mar" ("Supreme Ruler of the Earth and Sea"), was known as the Iturbidista faction. A third group was republican. The republican group was committed to constitutional rule without an emperor, king, or military chief.

The poor, the mestizos, Indians, mulattos, and blacks were mostly unrepresented in the new government. The old revolutionaries—Nicolás Bravo, Vicente Guerrero, Guadalupe Victoria—had split with Iturbide after they realized that his vision of independence had little in common with their vision of revolution.

As Iturbide probably expected, King Ferdinand VII was not inclined to live in Mexico, even as its emperor. Iturbide in fact thought that he himself was the most

likely, if not the only, candidate to head the new nation.

Congress apparently thought otherwise. They were suspicious of Iturbide and of his desire for power. The congress began to legislate restrictions on the power of the head of the military as well as a decrease in the size of the military. Iturbide clashed with the congress over and over again. They fought over such matters as whether Iturbide or the president of congress would occupy the body's highest seat, and whether Iturbide could

In 1821, Spain's representative, Juan O'Donojú, signed the treaty that recognized Mexico's independence.

After winning Mexico's independence from Spain, Iturbide set his sights on a Mexican monarchy.

unsheathe his sword during congressional sessions. In May, tensions came to a head. Pío Marcha, a sergeant in Iturbide's old regiment, led his comrades into the streets of Mexico City to proclaim Iturbide as Emperor Agustín I. Mobs suddenly appeared in the streets, supporting the proclamation. Simultaneous lighting of public buildings made clear that the movement was well planned. It worked.

By noon of the next day, Iturbide had accepted the crown offered by the military. The congress was surrounded by a threatening mob. Though seventy-four members of congress were absent from the session, sixty-seven members voted to name Iturbide emperor of Mexico. Fifteen voted to delay the decision until the provinces could be consulted. The opposition was overpowered. By this vote, Iturbide was named emperor of Mexico.

5 Independence for Whom?

Under the leadership of Agustín Iturbide, Mexico had won its independence from Spain. Almost immediately, however, the old divisions within the revolutionary movement reappeared. Most notable were the political heirs of Hidalgo, who saw independence as the way to free mestizos, Indians, blacks, and mulattos from legal discrimination. The followers of Hidalgo had joined Iturbide when he called for independence. Though he welcomed their help in winning independence, it was quickly apparent that he did not want to share power with them after independence was won.

Iturbide had envisioned a Mexican empire, with himself and his descendants reigning as hereditary monarchs. In Iturbide's vision, Mexico would rule over the smaller Central American nations to the south. His grand plan was a royalist vision, hardly revolutionary at all. Instead of a Spanish monarchy ruling from across the Atlantic, Iturbide proposed a Creole monarchy ruling from Mexico City. Soon Iturbide reached for more

In a lavish ceremony, Iturbide, taking the new name of Agustín I, becomes emperor of Mexico. Iturbide had plans to use his position to create a Mexican empire.

power than even his Creole allies were willing to give him.

Iturbide and congress quickly moved to define the new monarchy. Congress named Iturbide's father "Prince of the Union," awarded his sister the title of Princess, and made the monarchy hereditary. In July 1822, a grand coronation was performed, complete with anointing by a bishop and imperial crowns for both the emperor and empress. In addition to a palace, the new imperial family was given the services of a majordomo, or head steward, a captain of the guard, bishops and chaplains and preachers, gentlemen of the chamber, pages, personal physicians and surgeons, and maids of honor.

The new emperor, Agustín I, was promptly recognized by Nicolás Bravo and Vicente Guerrero. Neither seemed envious of his high position. Guerrero sent a message telling the new emperor that he was confident that the liberator would not become a tyrant. If his words were a warning, they went unheeded.

Mexican Revolution Leads the Way for Central American Independence

Although Mexico was Spain's largest colony, the revolt against colonial rule spread far beyond its borders. When Iturbide created for himself an imperial throne, such Latin American liberators as

Uniting All Mexicans?

In Iturbide of Mexico, *William Spence Robertson describes Iturbide setting out his appeal for unity across the divisive lines of race in his preamble to the Plan of Iguala. He may not have considered that Indian Mexicans would feel excluded by his claim that all Mexicans were "of Spanish descent."*

"European Spaniards! Mexico is your country, for you live there. In it are your beloved wives and your tender children, your haciendas, your commerce, and your other possessions. Mexicans! who among you can say that you are not of Spanish descent? Behold the delicate chain which unites us; consider the other bonds of friendship, education, language, interdependence of interests, and the harmony of sentiment, and you will realize that the general happiness of the Kingdom requires that all its people should be united in one opinion and in one voice. The time has arrived when you should show a uniformity of sentiment and should make known that our union is the powerful hand which emancipates Mexico from foreign rule. At the head of a valiant and resolute army, I have proclaimed Mexican independence."

Simon Bolívar sent congratulatory and admiring messages. Central American countries did even more: Some were ready to become part of a new empire, ruled from Mexico City.

Honduras and Nicaragua had proclaimed their independence from Spain in September 1821. Guatemala achieved independence by the end of October. A delegation of Guatemalan leaders wrote to Iturbide that his "glorious achievements" led to the triumph of their patriots and the achievement of independence without shedding a single drop of blood.

> The proclamation of independence which your Excellency made at Iguala did not discourage discontented persons. The government tried to increase their confidence in itself by issuing a proclamation which treated the person of your Excellency with disdain and by spreading reports which were contrary to the accounts that reached us about your glorious achievements. This progress rejoiced the hearts of those who favored independence. Our papers spread the news in Central America with such happy results that by the thirtieth of the next month not a single drop of blood had been shed in support of our independence.[26]

El Salvador declared its independence from Spain and its union with the Mexican empire early in 1822. Once in power, Iturbide sent troops to Central America, assuring that the United Provinces of Central America, newly independent from Spain, would now be part of the Mexican empire.

Trouble at Home for the Emperor

When Emperor Agustín I took his throne, the government was struggling with severe financial problems. Paying both the Spanish soldiers who were waiting to return home and the revolutionary soldiers who had won independence drained the treasury. The new nation also inherited a huge public debt from the viceroyalty. Mines, haciendas, and towns had been devastated by more than a decade of war.

Both the congress and the new emperor looked to merchants and the church for cash, but many wealthy merchants decided to take their money and leave for Spain rather than stay on and face either taxes or forced loans. Iturbide actually lowered taxes, but this only worsened the financial crisis, leaving the government with even less money to operate. As the government tried to negotiate a loan from England, it alienated the church with more demands for money.

Congress showed some independence, wanting at the very least to share in the task of government and in making decisions. Emperor Agustín insisted on having the ultimate authority. His power came from the military, not from winning elections. He did not want to listen to congress, let alone share power with it. By the end of October, the emperor had dissolved congress and imprisoned dozens of its leaders.

The United States had recognized the newly independent country on its southern border. Now U.S. president James Monroe sent Joel R. Poinsett to Mexico to assess the situation there. Regarding the emperor, Poinsett reported:

His usurpation of the chief authority has been the most glaring and unjustifiable; and his exercise of power arbitrary and tyrannical. With a pleasing address and prepossessing exterior, and by lavish profusion, he has attached the officers and soldiers to his person, and so long as he possesses the means of paying and rewarding them, so long will he maintain himself

The Triumph of Iturbide

Many welcomed the establishment of a monarchy and the reign of Emperor Agustín Iturbide I, as reported by Hubert Howe Bancroft in History of Mexico.

"Thus Iturbide triumphed at last. But it was a triumph without dignity or the lustre of greatness. It was a triumph won by trickery, through the medium of rough soldiery and the hoarse cries of a rabble. Yet it cannot be said that his elevation was unacceptable to the nation. The dilatory proceedings, first of the provisional junta and then of the congress, had exhausted the patience of the people. . . . Discontent and indignation were the consequences, and the nation was ready for a change. Nor was it unnatural that the people should look for aid to him who had been their liberator. . . .

The monarchy was decreed hereditary, and the succession secured to his eldest son, on whom was conferred the title of prince imperial. His family was made royal, his sons and daughters being styled Mexican princes and princesses, and his father entitled the prince of the union."

Many people, frustrated with the state of the country, welcomed the reign of Emperor Agustín I.

In 1822, General Antonio López de Santa Anna (pictured) rebelled against Iturbide and called for a new constitutional government.

supported the empire, but nursed his own ambitions. When the emperor ordered Santa Anna removed from his command in Veracruz, Santa Anna refused to leave. Rallying his troops, he declared instead that Iturbide had violated the provisions of his own Plan of Iguala. Santa Anna reminded his troops and his fellow citizens of the Three Guarantees, which had been the basis of Iturbide's revolt against Spain. Now Santa Anna called for a constitutional government based on religion, independence, and unity.

Two old revolutionaries, General Bravo and General Guerrero, declared their support for Santa Anna. Much of the army also backed him. In March, after less than nine months on the throne, Emperor Agustín I abdicated.

End of Empire

When Iturbide was deposed, the Central American countries went their own way, declaring independence from Mexico on July 1, 1823. Although all agreed to a federal constitution, the elites of each country vied for control. Liberals wanted a stronger central government. Conservatives wanted greater autonomy for each country and continuing control by their own Spanish and Creole elites. The different factions clashed continually.

A Honduran hero, Francisco Morazán, led a victorious army that held the provinces together until 1838. Opposition from the church and from conservative elites eventually defeated Morazán, however, and the union fell apart.

England stood ready to step into whatever role Spain left vacant in Latin

on the throne; when these fail he will be precipitated from it.[27]

Meanwhile, Spain had rejected the treaty signed by O'Donojú and refused to recognize Mexican independence. Spanish loyalists still held one key fort, San Juan de Ulúa, in the crucial port of Veracruz.

In November 1822, the emperor turned his attention to this remaining military stumbling block. Leaving the troubled capital, Agustín I marched toward Veracruz. Stopping at the town of Jalapa, he demanded an explanation for the hold-out fort from the commander of the Mexican troops in Veracruz, General Antonio López de Santa Anna.

Santa Anna, like Iturbide, had been a royalist officer. He gave his allegiance to the Army of the Three Guarantees and

America. In Central America, England invested in railroads and government securities. It also seized territory that it called British Honduras (now the independent country of Belize), and territory on Nicaragua's Mosquito Coast.

Governing Mexico After Iturbide

With Iturbide gone, the congress reconvened. Its members formally declared that Mexico could now adopt any constitution that it wanted. The congress also gave Iturbide a pension, conditioned on his living

Though Honduran hero Francisco Morazán fought to keep the union of Central American countries together after Iturbide was deposed, opposition from the church and conservative elites soon caused the union to fall apart.

in Italy. By doing so, they hoped to keep him away from Mexico and out of Mexican politics forever.

Then the congress appointed a provisional government headed by a triumvirate of Generals Guadalupe Victoria, Nicolás Bravo, and Pedro Negrete, a Spaniard who had declared loyalty to Mexico. This executive trio named a four-person cabinet, including Lucas Alamán, a wealthy and conservative Creole just returned from Spain. By including leaders with a wide range of political beliefs, the new government hoped to unify the country and win the support of all Mexicans.

Next, the congress proceeded to frame a constitution providing for an independent and federal republic. The provinces would be united but each would still maintain its own identity and government. Power was divided between congress and the president of the United Mexican States. Roman Catholicism was declared the official religion of the country, and all other religious practice was prohibited. The Constitution of 1824 was the first comprehensive attempt to set up an independent Mexican government.

While the congress was organizing the new constitution and government, Iturbide decided to return from Italy. False friends told him that the disarray in Mexico meant that he would be welcomed and reinstated as emperor. Instead, he was executed on July 19, 1824.

The first president under the new constitution was Guadalupe Victoria, a veteran of Hidalgo's revolution. Politically, Victoria was a Federalist, or Liberal. His vice president was another old revolutionary, General Nicolás Bravo, who was a Centralist, or Conservative, in political allegiance.

On command, a firing squad executes Iturbide, who had just returned from exile with expectations of a triumphal return to the throne.

Political Divisions in Mexico

Political parties, as they exist in the twentieth century, were not a part of the political scene of the early nineteenth century in Mexico. To be a Federalist or Liberal meant to share a general belief in a less centralized form of government. Under Iturbide, this faction had been called "republican." Adherents supported a government that was a federation of the provinces or states of Mexico.

If they had a defined political philosophy, Liberals shared the ideals of the French and American Revolutions. They believed in independence, in political liberties, and also in more egalitarian rela-

tions between classes and races. The support for this tendency came largely from mestizos and from some Creoles, as well. Both Liberals and Conservatives shared a belief in elected government and national independence.

The other side had been known under Iturbide as Bourbonist or Iturbidista. The Bourbonist faction wanted a return to monarchy, with a European monarch ruling the Mexican empire. The Iturbidista faction wanted a monarchy under the Iturbide dynasty.

After Iturbide was deposed and a republic was declared, everyone on the Mexican political scene claimed to be a republican, so political labels changed. Now the former Bourbonists were called

Betraying the Republic

After switching sides—from supporting the Spanish rule of Mexico to fighting for its independence— Iturbide showed his true allegiance remained to himself. Hubert Howe Bancroft, in his History of Mexico, *says Iturbide was not willing to see the establishment of a republic that he did not rule.*

"During the elections Iturbide had not remained idle. His agents had been everywhere active in their endeavors to secure the appointment of representatives who would support his views. They had only been partially successful, however; the liberals had shown equal energy in their labors, and a number of truly patriotic and enlightened men had been elected. Though the congress would not be so favorably composed as he had intended, the generalissimo had still a resource left by which he hoped to cramp the proceedings of the opposing party— namely, intimidation. A display of military force would effect this, and under such circumstances a form of oath could be exacted that would fetter free action. He was determined that the nation's representatives should not decide for it its form of government. They should be compelled to swear to observe the plan of Iguala. It was a monstrous insult to the dignity of a nation, the liberty of which he had so lately proclaimed, to prescribe its government, and impose law upon the assembly appointed to frame its constitution."

Centralists. They advocated a strong and centralized government. The former Iturbidista faction split between Federalists and Centralists. The Centralists drew support from the wealthy classes, the military (particularly former royalists), and the church.

Economic and political divisions within the country threatened it from the very beginning. Independence from Spain had been achieved, but there was not yet a consensus on what form that independence should take.

Complete freedom of the press allowed open debate by the various political factions. Plotting against the government continued from many sides. Impatient with President Victoria's seeming weakness in the face of dissent and plots, General Bravo revolted against the government in which he served as vice president. He was defeated by General Vicente Guerrero, who ran for president in 1828.

Guerrero, a champion of the people, lost by a narrow margin to a former Iturbide follower, General Gómez Pedraza, whose support came from the upper classes. Another revolution followed the election, this one led by a radical journalist from the Yucatán, Lorenzo Zavala. General Santa Anna took up arms in support of Zavala and Guerrero. When the dust settled, Guerrero took office as president in April 1828. Zavala served in his cabinet as minister of the treasury, and a former royalist officer, General Anastasio Bustamante, was vice president.

Some of the divisions in political leadership were based on differences between economic classes. Political leaders were also divided in their attitudes toward the church and religion. While the constitution had established Roman Catholicism as the official religion of Mexico, church wealth remained an issue.

The church still owned large amounts of property and held far more wealth than did the various governments of Mexico. Some church property was held by the state. Should this property be returned to the church, kept by the state, or sold to pay debts and raise money for government operations? Could the church be taxed? Should it in some way be made to contribute to the expense of governing and reconstructing the war-torn country?

The church itself was divided. Much of the hierarchy was conservative, but many of the lower-ranking clergy had supported the revolution. Indeed, many had fought in it and hundreds had been executed for their part in it.

Where did religious loyalty lie? Did religious people owe support to the government of, for example, Guerrero and Zavala? Or should they oppose it because Guerrero and Zavala had seized power outside the constitutional process? Should they support the government because it was helping poor people? Or should they oppose the government, because it took church property to do so?

The Guerrero Presidency

When Guerrero became president, treasury minister Zavala found the treasury empty and public debt mounting. He quickly instituted new measures to raise money. Zavala ordered the sale of church properties, already held by the government for decades. He also instituted income taxes for the first time, proposing a tax plan that was carefully graduated so that the wealthy would pay and the poor would not. These measures alienated the church and angered the upper classes. According to historian Jan Bazant, "This was perhaps the only Mexican government of the nineteenth century which attempted to benefit the common people and to establish what would be called later a democracy; the only time in Mexican history up to the present century that the government favored the poor over the rich."[28]

If Guerrero and Zavala had only had to deal with financial crises, their government might have survived. That was not to be the case. In 1829, the Spanish army under a General Barrada landed, making an attempt to retake Mexico. General Santa Anna quickly drove the Spanish army out of Mexico, in so doing becoming a national hero.

The political focus shifted to attacks on Zavala and his tax proposals. Vice President and General Anastasio Bustamante revolted in December, with the open support of Nicolás Bravo and at least silent support from Santa Anna. Bustamante took the presidency in January 1829. President Guerrero retired to his hacienda and Minister of the Treasury Zavala left for exile in the United States. In 1831,

Guerrero emerged to lead a revolt against Bustamante and was betrayed, captured, and executed.

With military coup following coup, various players occupied the political stage. Lucas Alamán, conservative Creole secretary of state under Bustamante, was one prominent figure. Under his leadership, the Bustamante regime closed dissenting newspapers, got rid of Federalist state governors, and tried to restrict congress and protect the wealthy. Soon General Santa Anna led yet another revolt, this time in favor of federalism and against Bustamante. His coup placed General Gómez Pedraza in the presidency in 1832. The next year Santa Anna himself was elected president.

Whatever his faults (and they were many), Santa Anna was a skillful politi-

General Anastasio Bustamante (pictured) held the presidency for nearly three years until a revolt by Santa Anna forced him out of office.

cian. "He was a profound judge of men, with a keen insight into the human character, generally with his fingers on the public pulse," writes historian Ramón Eduardo Ruiz. "He spent his entire political life making war, raising money and plotting. When out of office, he plotted to get in; when in office, he plotted to stay there."[29]

The Santa Anna era was marked by greed and corruption, both attributes of the general himself. A popular saying called him a man with the face of Caesar and the mind of a rogue. He had no fixed political commitments and his only loyalty was to himself.

A royalist officer, he embraced the insurgency and fawned on Iturbide, hailing his "sublime" imperial pretensions, then acclaimed the banners of the Republic. During the 1820s, he was a Federalist, a sympathizer of the Yorquinos and Guerrero. In 1832, after allying himself with the cuartelazo [coup] against Bustamante, he helped bring back Gómez Pedraza, before winning the presidency as a Liberal, an admirer of the constitution. Then he swung over to the camp of its critics, became a Centralist by 1843 and a dictator the next year, only to be an ally of the apostles of "constitutionalism" by 1846, ending his political career as a dictator. Once more seeking the blessings of public applause, he offered his sword to the French invaders of Mexico in the 1860s; rejected, he swore allegiance to the Republicans, who disdained his offer.[30]

As one coup followed another, divisions within Mexico continued. Rural and urban Mexicans had differing interests,

Santa Anna ran an administration fraught with greed and corruption.

with much of rural Mexico wanting the greater independence and self-government promised to the provinces by the Federalists. Wealthier and urban Mexicans often preferred the Centralist model, as they could wield greater power in a more centralized government. As the industrial revolution came to Mexico, an urban working class developed. The interests of these workers were different from both those of the peasants and those of the wealthy landowners and merchants.

Race, too, continued to divide Mexicans. Creoles, now solidly in power, no longer suffered from a spurious racial distinction. Creoles, however, were not ready to concede social and political equality to mestizos. Despite legal guarantees of equality, Indians were not treated as full citizens. Racism provided a continuing rationale for oppression.

From top to bottom of the social scale, the color of one's skin influenced personal and class relations. As before, money and education "whitened" the skin but not entirely. How much this prejudice poisoned relationships between individuals and groups in society, no one really knows; but no one doubts that it did.

By the 1850s, Mexico's heterogeneous society had approximately eight million inhabitants, over half of them persons of dark skins, largely because of Indian ancestry. A small population of mulattoes further darkened the country's complexion. Most persons "of color" . . . inhabited the countryside; whites, perhaps a million, dwelt in the cities. . . . Although an oligarchy of whites ruled the roost, a mestizo universe toiled beneath it. The shaky social pyramid rested on a bronze base, with mestizos exploiting Indians and both criollos and light-skinned mestizos of the upper strata riding herd over both.[31]

The first decades of independence brought little benefit to darker-skinned Mexicans, or to poor Mexicans, whether they were agricultural or industrial laborers.

6 Texas and the Mexican-American War

From the north, a powerful neighbor looked eagerly at Mexico's sparsely settled border territories. Beginning in colonial times, U.S. citizens had settled throughout the vast expanse of northern Mexico. Now that Mexico was independent of Spain, the settlers moved to become independent of Mexico. They could do so only with the backing of the United States.

The Monroe Doctrine Sets U.S. Policy

The influence and intervention of the United States in Mexican affairs began as soon as the Spanish colonial regime ended. Mexicans already felt uneasy about the intentions and actions of their powerful northern neighbor. A Mexican proverb laments that the country is *tan lejos de Dios, tan cerca de los Estados Unidos*—so far from God and so near to the United States.

After winning its own independence from England, the United States feared the expansion of English influence in the hemisphere. To forestall this, U.S. president James Monroe promulgated the Monroe Doctrine, which asserted that the entire hemisphere belonged within an American sphere of influence. Through

President Monroe, the United States claimed the right to intervene anywhere that European countries presented a threat.

U.S. president James Monroe asserted that the Monroe Doctrine gave the United States the right to intervene in foreign affairs.

In the spirit of manifest destiny, a pioneer family makes a trek to Texas, where they hope to claim land.

The Monroe Doctrine grew out of the political philosophy known as manifest destiny. Manifest destiny is the name given to the belief that the United States had a right and duty to expand its borders from sea to sea. Even before the United States had established its own independent government, Thomas Jefferson looked to its eventual control of Latin America. "The Virginian's growing concern about expanding U.S. power," writes historian Walter LaFeber, led him "to decide that it would be better if the Spanish held on to their territory 'till our population can be sufficiently advanced to gain it from them piece by piece.'"[32]

In the early nineteenth century, England, France, and the United States were the major players on the international scene. As Spain's colonies won their independence from a mother country weakened by war and economic difficulties, these players watched vigilantly from the sidelines. Each was poised to seize any opportunities for economic profit and political power.

Settling Texas: Setting the Stage for the Mexican-American War

The border between the viceroyalty of New Spain and the United States was set by the Adams-Onís Treaty of 1819. Mexican territory stretched north through much of the present-day United States, including Texas, New Mexico, and California. The independent Mexican republic inherited the same boundaries.

U.S. pioneer Stephen Austin led hundreds of colonists into Texas, which was then a part of Mexico.

The northern territories of California, New Mexico, and Texas were sparsely settled. Facing an expansionist United States, the Spanish government had tried to establish settlements there. It even granted generous concessions to settlers from the United States.

One beneficiary was Moses Austin, who was permitted to settle three hundred families from the United States in Texas. Each family was granted one thousand acres, plus one hundred for each child and eighty for each slave.

Austin, who became a Spanish citizen, and his settlers had to meet conditions designed to protect Spain and Mexico. They were required to become Catholics. They also had to settle away from the coast and

the U.S.-Mexico border. They agreed to swear allegiance to Spain. They were allowed to bring their slaves, but not to sell them. Children born to the slaves would be free men and women.

Moses Austin died before leading the settlers into Texas. Then the Spanish government ended with the installation of Iturbide as emperor. Austin's son Stephen inherited the concession, upheld by Iturbide, and led the settlers into Texas. Before long, land speculators and colonists from the United States effectively took control of the settlement of the northern territories. Given the turmoil of the central Mexican government, that was an easy matter. By 1825, only thirty-five hundred of twenty-five thousand residents of Texas were Mexicans.

The independent-minded U.S. settlers had no intention of complying with the terms of their concessions. Many settlements were made up of trespassers who had no legal claim to live in Mexico at all. They ignored the religious requirements, spoke no Spanish, and remained loyal to the United States. When Mexico abolished slavery in 1829, the settlers protested so vehemently that enforcement of the law was suspended.

In 1830, fearing a takeover of the northern provinces by the United States and the unruly settlers, Mexico passed a law forbidding further settlements by U.S. citizens. In response, angry settlers called a meeting in Anáhuac, since renamed Galveston. They barred Mexican residents of Texas from the meeting, then voted to demand that Mexico City remove its customhouses and grant statehood to Texas. This would leave Texas as part of Mexico, but as an equal state within the republic, despite its small population.

Meanwhile, the U.S. ambassador to Mexico, Joel Poinsett, proposed to the government in Mexico City that the United States buy Texas. His proposal proved so unpopular that he was recalled to Washington and replaced by Anthony Butler. Butler repeated the same proposal. He also began pushing for payments by Mexico to U.S. citizens who claimed damage to their property in Mexico.

War with Texas

As U.S. settlers plotted against the Mexican government, they recruited more settlers and mercenaries to their side. U.S. neutrality laws forbade its citizens from participating in foreign wars, and the Mexican government asked Washington to enforce its laws. The U.S. government

Forming Political Parties

Political parties were greatly influenced by the fraternal connections that people had made through freemasonry. The various masonic associations attracted people of differing political convictions, according to Jan Bazant in A Concise History of Mexico from Hidalgo to Cárdenas.

"The pro-Hispanic bourbonists were associated with freemasons of the Scottish rite; as such, they were called 'Scottish Rite Masons.' They were the core out of which the conservatives would rise in the future. Now that a republic was becoming an established fact, monarchism began to be seen as treasonable; hence, everyone now called himself a republican. And as all were now republicans, new distinctions were needed. So the bourbonists became 'centralists,' followers of a strong central regime. The anti-Hispanic republicans became 'federalists,' favoring a federation on the United States model. The capital city had been identified with the viceroyalty and the different revolutionary currents had been strongest in the provinces. This continued after independence, and as the progressives' stronghold lay in the provinces, they naturally argued for a high degree of provincial autonomy. Later, this group would transform themselves into liberals but, as political parties were as yet unknown, a suitable archetype was needed; it was found in freemasonry. Thus, in 1825 the federalists—with the help of [diplomat Joel] Poinsett, now American minister to Mexico—succeeded in organizing lodges of the York rite; and so the federalists became known as 'York Rite Masons.'"

ignored the arming of settlers and the recruiting of mercenary soldiers.

The rebels named William B. Travis as governor of Texas; Sam Houston became commander in chief of a provisional Texan army.

General Santa Anna pledged to march on the rebels and crush them. He mortgaged his own hacienda to raise funds for an army, then began his march at the beginning of 1836.

On February 2, Santa Anna's army set off for Texas by way of Monclova, a town in Coahuila; the winter weather was cold, and more so for Santa Anna's soldiers, nearly all of them from the warm climates of Mexico. In late February 1836, the army, such as it was, reached Texas. At El Alamo, just outside of San Antonio, it found Travis with 146 men barricaded in an old Franciscan church, determined to "win or die." Unwilling to take on Santa Anna's army, Houston and his men had retreated before the advance of the Mexicans, leaving Travis to face the music alone. On March 6, the Mexicans attacked, scaled the walls of the old church, and, fighting man to man, took it. "Travis," according to the diary of [a] Mexican soldier, "died bravely"; Jim Bowie, the second in command, "like a coward." Every defender perished, save for a boy of fourteen, two women, and the black slave of Travis. Mexican losses, much heavier, totaled 400 dead and countless

A nineteenth-century lithograph depicts the 1836 Battle of the Alamo, where all of the Texan defenders lost their lives during the lengthy siege by Santa Anna's troops.

wounded. "Another victory such as this one," the Mexican chronicler wrote, "and we will lose the war."[33]

Santa Anna turned to pursue Sam Houston's army. Unfortunately for him, he caught the Texans forty-six days later. Praising the bravery of their fighters, Texans rallied to the cry of "Remember the Alamo!" Sam Houston decisively defeated Santa Anna at the Battle of San Jacinto, taking him prisoner. While in Houston's custody, Santa Anna signed treaties acknowledging the end of the conflict. He agreed to seek his government's recognition of Texan independence. Mexico refused to give it, but lacked the money and resources needed to reconquer the new Lone Star Republic.

Freed by the Texans, Santa Anna soon had another opportunity to recover his reputation. After a gang of soldiers ransacked a French pastry shop in Mexico City, France demanded reparations. Mexico did not, and perhaps could not, pay. In 1838, the French invaded Veracruz, a limited invasion that became known as the Pastry War. Santa Anna marched off to Veracruz. He lost a leg in the fighting but drove out the French. Santa Anna returned in triumph to Mexico City and high office, carrying with him the leg he had lost, which he buried with pomp and ceremony. In 1844, however, Santa Anna was deposed again and exiled to Cuba.

Hostilities between Mexico and the breakaway republic of Texas continued intermittently until 1846. In the decade following rebellion, Texas called itself an independent republic, although it was clear that most of its citizens wanted to be part of the United States. The U.S. government, uneasily holding together slave and free states, both wanted and feared annexation of Texas, where slavery was permitted.

United States Annexes Texas

Proponents of manifest destiny believed that God intended the United States to expand from the Atlantic to the Pacific. They were convinced that not only Texas but also California and even Baja California should be annexed. Nevertheless, the free states were not eager to add another slave state to the Union. Antislavery politicians may also have seen the bitter irony of endorsing Texan secession from the Mexican republic while arguing against southern slave states' secession from the United States.

In 1844, James Polk won the presidency on a platform that included the annexation of Texas. Outgoing president John Tyler, a slaveholder from Virginia, pushed annexation of Texas through Congress before stepping down. In July 1845, Texas agreed to be annexed.

The Mexican ambassador warned Washington that annexation would mean war. In a show of force, the United States sent its army into Texas and positioned a navy unit off the coast of California, prepared to land in California after U.S. agents stirred Californians' demands for independence from Mexico.

Mexico was in no shape to fight a war, but when the United States sent a minister plenipotentiary to Mexico City to negotiate a settlement, the terms he brought were considered entirely unacceptable. According to the settlement, Mexico would accept both the annexation of

Santa Anna

Ramón Eduardo Ruiz, in Triumph and Tragedy: A History of the Mexican People, *reports that Santa Anna ruled Mexico, on and off, for decades. Although his military leadership was often unsuccessful, he managed to retreat to his hacienda when out of favor, and then to return to power when the next crisis loomed.*

"In 1833, Santa Anna was just thirty-six years of age. Of medium height, more slender than fat, this criollo from Veracruz was fair of skin but of sallow complexion. Women found him 'gentlemanly' and 'good-looking.' He could be charming, spicing his conversation with the *jarocho* accent of his native Veracruz; although neither a glutton nor a connoisseur of food, he enjoyed holding forth on the virtues of the fare on the table, discussing in detail the seasoning of a dish, how to prepare oysters, octopus, and so on. Intellectually an illiterate, for he never read, Santa Anna spoke a bastard Spanish enlivened by words foreign to it. He was a profound judge of men, with a keen insight into the human character, generally with his fingers on the public pulse. He spent 'his entire political life making war, raising money and plotting.' When out of office, he plotted to get in; when in office, he plotted to stay there.

Santa Anna loved to gamble, especially to play cards, and, when the occasion permitted, to woo women. He was a bit of a Don Juan: 'His Excellency,' remembered Madame Calderón de la Barca, 'is by no means indifferent to beauty—*tout au contraire.*' Cockfights were his chief pleasure; he never neglected to care for his gamecocks at his hacienda, Manga de Clavo. At the cockfights in Mexico City, which he attended faithfully, he knew by name every fine gamecock. At these events, he was their elixir, ready to fix odds, collect bets, and wager himself, while mixing freely with the rabble. At thirty years of age, he married María Inés de la Paz García, the daughter of Spaniards, and spent his honeymoon at Manga de Clavo, where he found solace when fate betrayed him."

Santa Anna ruled Mexico as president eleven times between 1833 and 1855.

U.S. troops storm the Mexican city of Monterrey, setting into motion the war between the United States and Mexico.

Texas and payment of $40 million for the territory north of the Rio Grande to the Nueces River and for northern New Mexico and California.

Mexican president José Joaquín Herrera knew that selling half of the nation would be political suicide, but, knowing also that Mexico did not have the military or economic strength to win a war with the United States, he opposed war. A military coup followed in December 1845, led by General Mariano Paredes Arrillaga. The new leader of the country swore to defend Mexico at all costs. U.S. military units kept maneuvering closer to Mexico.

> On the banks of the Río Bravo [the Rio Grande], [General Zachary] Taylor erected a fort across from the town of Matamoros, ignoring cries of alarm from the Mexicans. When General Pedro de Ampudia, the Mexican commander, demanded that he withdraw, Taylor, instead, ordered American warships to blockade the mouth of the Río Bravo, cutting off the supply route

for Matamoros. "We do not have a particle of right to be here," confessed an American colonel with Taylor; "it looks as if the government sent a small force on purpose to bring on a war, as to have a pretext to take California."[34]

War with the United States

In the spring of 1846 the war began, and U.S. troops poured into Mexico. U.S. invaders marched into New Mexico and California. Troops landed in Monterey and San Francisco, California. Others crossed the Rio Grande and conquered the northeastern Mexican cities of Monterrey and Saltillo. Another naval unit landed in Veracruz.

At the same time, intrigue and internal battles escalated in the government in Mexico City. Santa Anna was now back from exile and professing to be a Federalist. Creole leaders threw out Paredes Arrillaga and replaced him with Santa Anna. When congress confiscated church property to finance the war, a group of officers revolted. The rebels fought with soldiers loyal to the government instead of marching together to meet the U.S. invaders.

Once again, Santa Anna marched to war. This time his poorly equipped troops died by the thousands on their way to battle. Nearly fifteen hundred died in the single battle at La Angostura. Yet more died in retreat.

The U.S. Army continued to attack from several directions. Eventually, it occupied Mexico City, where it demanded that Mexico give up half of its territory in return for $15 million and forgiveness of the claims made against Mexico by U.S. citizens.

Many Mexicans were outraged by the demand for surrender and sale of the national territory. They wanted to continue to fight.

Mexico Pays a High Price for Peace

The Creole-run government had but one alternative—to call on the people to wage a prolonged guerrilla war against the occupying armies of the United States. That might have worked. Fighting on might have saved at least some of the Mexican national territory and much of its national pride. But such a call would have meant a shift in power from the Creole elites to the masses of the Mexican people. That shift

U.S. troops easily overtake Veracruz as part of the effort to expand U.S. territory.

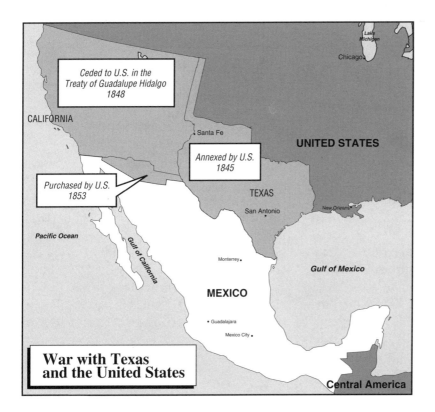

War with Texas and the United States

Map labels: Ceded to U.S. in the Treaty of Guadalupe Hidalgo 1848 — Annexed by U.S. 1845 — Purchased by U.S. 1853 — CALIFORNIA — Santa Fe — UNITED STATES — Lake Michigan — Chicago — TEXAS — San Antonio — New Orleans — Pacific Ocean — Gulf of California — Monterrey — Gulf of Mexico — MEXICO — Guadalajara — Mexico City — Central America

of power seemed far worse to the Creoles than capitulation to the superior military might of the United States. Despite opposition by many Mexicans, the majority of the Creoles meeting at Querétaro agreed to the U.S. terms for peace.

In fact, the Creole elite faced an internal revolt at that very moment. Mayan Indians in the southernmost province of Yucatán had long suffered at the hands of the white sugar and henequen [fiber crop used for twine] plantation owners. In what became known as the Caste War, they revolted against their oppressors. By 1848, the Mayans were close to victory.

The Creoles of Yucatán wrote to Washington, Madrid, and London, seeking help against the Mayans. In return, the Creoles offered to give sovereignty over the Yucatán to any foreign government that saved them. Although their request was rejected, the Creoles happily welcomed occupying U.S. Marines, and the lands were transferred in the Treaty of Guadalupe Hidalgo in 1848. The Creoles of Mexico City used part of the money received for the sale of Mexican lands to pay for guns for the Yucatán. By selling part of Mexico's land, they preserved their political control of the remaining territory.

7 Debt and War

Between 1833 and 1855, Santa Anna held the office of president eleven times. Santa Anna's on-and-off dominance of the Mexican political scene even outlasted his defeat in the Mexican-American War. When Santa Anna agreed to the Gadsden Purchase—the sale of the Mesilla, now part of southern Arizona—to the United States in 1853, however, he sealed his doom. Infuriated by this betrayal of Mexican sovereignty, a motley crew of civilians led a revolt against Santa Anna. While the military remained loyal to the general, they were defeated in the Revolution of Ayutla. Liberals then began La Reforma—the reform.

Over the next decade, La Reforma would lead to changes in the constitution and laws of Mexico, all with the goal of giving increased voice and power to the poor. La Reforma ended after a bloody civil war and the French conquest of a devastated Mexico.

Leaders of La Reforma

La Reforma was led by three prominent Liberal politicians: Melchor Ocampo, Benito Juárez, and Miguel Lerdo. Each developed his commitment to change as a result of his life experience. Their paths joined in New Orleans, where each had been sent into exile as a result of his political beliefs.

Melchor Ocampo was born in Michoacán in about 1814. He was an illegitimate child, raised by an elderly lady. At

Melchor Ocampo, one of the three leaders of La Reforma, called for social reforms and justice for the poor.

her death, Ocampo inherited her hacienda. Although he now owned an estate, Ocampo still believed strongly in justice for the poor. He ran his hacienda according to his beliefs. At that time, debt was used to keep peasants as virtual slaves on haciendas. Ocampo refused to use this weapon against the peasants who worked for him. He repeatedly canceled the debts owed to him by his workers. His sympathy for the poor kept Ocampo from increasing his personal wealth.

Ocampo served as governor of Michoacán during the Mexican-American War. He opposed the peace treaty that ended the war, instead advocating guerrilla war against U.S. occupying forces. After the peace treaty was signed, he resigned the governor's position in protest.

Ocampo continued to speak out on issues of justice. In 1851, one of the laborers on his hacienda could not afford the church fee to bury his son. Angered, Ocampo made a speech to the Michoacán state congress. In his speech, he called for legal regulation of parish fees, and for lower fees. Ocampo's proposal led the church and conservatives to consider him an enemy. Ocampo was reelected governor of Michoacán in 1852. He began educational reforms, but was deposed and sent into exile in New Orleans.

Benito Juárez was another leader of La Reforma. He was the son of poor Indian parents who died when Juárez was still a child. As a child, he spoke only Zapotec, like the other Indians of his village. After moving to Oaxaca City at the age of twelve, he managed to get an education. From humble beginnings, Juárez became a lawyer and a politician. He was elected governor of the state of Oaxaca in 1847, at

Benito Juárez overcame adversity to become a powerful voice for land reform and the rights of the underprivileged.

the age of forty-one. In 1853, Santa Anna banished Benito Juárez from the country Juárez joined Ocampo in New Orleans. Until exile, Juárez had not been associated with a particular political ideology. While in New Orleans, he became a confirmed Liberal.

The third leader of La Reforma was Miguel Lerdo. Lerdo was born in Veracruz, the son of a Spanish merchant and a Creole mother. Lerdo became a friend of Santa Anna, who was also a native of Veracruz. Unlike Santa Anna, Lerdo was a committed Liberal and a critic of the church hierarchy.

New Constitution, New Laws

These three men began reforming the government, beginning with advocating free trade and capitalism. Although they were reformers, the Liberals were no revolutionaries.

Even Ignacio Ramírez, a man troubled by social inequalities, displayed no qualms in 1857, because "Mexican capitalists were not enemies of the working man." The charter's framers had not hesitated to write in guarantees for capitalists, as Ramírez explained, pointing out that nothing in it obligated the state to provide jobs, a principle enshrined just in Communist societies. Congress lacked the authority to dictate a "social revolution" and, besides that, "the country had no appetite for one." The right of labor recognized by the Constitution was "the freedom of the worker to look for a job."[35]

The Church and the Poor

The church that served the poor also lived on their backs. Melchor Ocampo was one of the most vocal advocates of reforming the system described here by Jan Bazant in A Concise History of Mexico from Hidalgo to Cárdenas.

"A frequent cause of illegitimacy among the lower class at that time was the high fee charged by parish priests for performing weddings. Fees for baptisms, marriages, and funerals provided the basic livelihood of curates [clergymen]. . . . The fee was so exorbitant for a wedding that many poor peasant couples never got married. However, resident peons—that is, laborers living on a hacienda—could normally get a loan from their employer to cover the marriage fee. . . . Some were able to extinguish their debt after a certain time, but most laborers remained in debt, especially if they had many children who obviously had to be baptized, some of whom died in infancy and also obviously had to be buried in consecrated ground. The result was a constant drain on the finances of most workers which perpetuated the peonage or debt-servitude, a system considered by enlightened farmers like Ocampo not only as immoral but as not conducive to progress. Ocampo himself canceled the full debt of his laborers four times, but he could not expect other landowners to follow his example. Considering the illegitimacy of his own birth, it is not surprising that this matter was close to Ocampo's heart."

A nineteenth-century painting depicts villagers entering a Catholic church in Mexico. La Reforma passed laws that regulated the amount of money churches could charge for performing such services as weddings, baptisms, and funerals.

Although they did not want to make a revolution, the Liberals did want to abolish many special privileges enjoyed by the church, the military, and the wealthy, and, predictably, they met with immediate opposition from those three powerful, conservative factions. Despite this opposition, the Liberal reformers pushed through a new constitution and three laws that formed the basis of La Reforma—the Ley Juárez, the Ley Lerdo, and the Ley Iglc sias, which regulated church fees, such as fees for baptisms, funerals, and weddings.

The principles on which the laws were based were also incorporated into the Constitution of 1857, which guaranteed constitutional government and individual rights. The new constitution provided for public schools, freedom of worship, and a free press. It also said that nuns and priests were free to give up their vows. Church authorities were outraged. Under the new constitution, they lost their previous monopoly on education. Now children could be educated without religious

influence. And they lost legal control of priests and nuns.

The Ley Juárez, named for its author, Benito Juárez, limited the power of the church and military *fueros*, or special courts exercising considerable political influence. Clergy and military were exempt from the regular civil and criminal courts. Members of the clergy could only be brought before clerical *fueros* and members of the military could only be brought before military *fueros*. This meant that civilians who had complaints against clergymen or military officials were at a decided disadvantage. A military judge was more likely to favor military officers who appeared before him. A church judge was more likely to favor priests over lay people.

The Ley Juárez did not attempt to abolish the *fueros*; rather, it proposed to limit their authority. Under the Ley Juárez, clerical *fueros* could try only matters concerning canon (church law). Military *fueros* could try only cases arising under military law. Civil and criminal cases against members of the clergy and military would henceforth be tried in the civil and criminal courts. That would put civilians on a more equal footing with the powerful clergy and military.

The Ley Lerdo, passed in 1856, was more complicated. Under this law, corporate holding of most property was prohibited. The law had a great impact on the church. As a corporation, the church had vast real estate holdings. The law allowed churches to keep church buildings and grounds, monasteries, and convents. It required them to sell all other lands. People living on church land were given the first opportunity to purchase it.

The church did not take the loss of its lands quietly. The archbishop of Mexico threatened to excommunicate Catholics who bought church property. The pope in Rome declared the Mexican laws null and void.

The Ley Lerdo also addressed ownership of land held for centuries in common by Indian villages, known as *ejidos*. *Ejido* land, farmed by the people of the village, was no one's to buy or sell. With the new law, to encourage the growth of small property holders, *ejidos* were to be sold to the people who lived on the land. If they chose not to buy the land, or if they had no money to buy it, the land could be sold to outsiders.

Indian communities often opposed the division of their communal lands. Wealthy individuals stood on the sidelines, ready to buy up any *ejido* that became available. At first, this happened when those who lived on the *ejido* failed to buy it, either because they opposed breaking up communal lands, because they did not understand their rights under the law, or because they had no money. Even when

they could purchase the land, new landowners often went into debt, either to buy farm supplies or because of family emergencies and illnesses, and then became vulnerable to foreclosure and loss of their land.

The actual impact of the Ley Lerdo was to increase concentration of land in the hands of the wealthy. Poor people living on the land often could not afford to buy even small farms. Large haciendas, which had belonged to the church or other corporations, were sold whole. Only the wealthy could buy them.

Rebellion Against La Reforma

As Indians and other poor farmers saw that the Ley Lerdo left them still landless, many prepared to resist.

> As before, the Indians did not take this lying down, some of them employed arms to defend their lands. Confronted with this widespread defiance, the Liberals declared that henceforth *ejido* parcels would be given only to their tillers. No longer was legislative intent to be left to chance; by receiving title to his parcel of land, the Indian would become the owner of private property. That, nonetheless, failed to halt entirely the acquisition of communal lands by greedy outsiders, who found the means to circumvent the law, at times, the record shows, by giving drunken Indians mescal [liquor] for their lands. How much land the Indians lost is a mystery, but that it was sizable most historians agree.[36]

Some Indians resisted La Reforma and the Ley Lerdo by armed rebellion. Soon military and church leaders joined in rebellion against the new constitution and the Liberal government. The country split over many issues.

Land-hungry ranchers chose the Liberal side, eager to keep open their opportunities to buy land under the Ley Lerdo. The church hierarchy, wanting to regain the privileges abolished by La Reforma, supported Conservatives. Many priests whose sympathies lay with the poor, not with the wealthy of their own church hierarchy, joined the Liberals. The army, stung by Liberal plans to reduce its size, sided with the Conservatives. Many Indians sat out the entire conflict, unhappy with both Conservative elitists and Liberal land reformers.

The splits were not simply political. Both military and guerrilla bands fought against the government, which responded by rallying loyal troops and citizens. Two bloody years of civil war followed, with battles raging throughout the countryside and destroying homes, crops, and businesses.

> The Guerra de la Reforma was a fratricidal conflict, besmirched by cruelty and killing on both sides. The Liberals started the atrocities by executing captive officers. Their rivals . . . went them one better, shooting civilians of Liberal stripe, lawyers particularly, whom they judged the mentors of the Reforma. By the middle of 1859, nearly all productive activity had come to a stop: fields lay untilled, commerce stagnated, contraband trade flourished, and bandits infested the countryside.[37]

Finally, the Liberals, led by Benito Juárez, emerged victorious. Juárez won the election of 1861 and resumed the presidency of a devastated and deeply indebted country.

The Economics of Independence

By the decade of La Reforma, Mexico owed debt it could not pay to England and France. Some was to have repaid loans made to finance wars. Some was acquired as loans made to develop industry or to keep the government afloat.

Debt to foreign banks was just one factor in the economics of independence. Much of Mexican industry was dependent on foreign trade. Now English investors bought, re-opened, and operated Mexican mines. Cheap, mass-produced English cotton flooded the Mexican market. Mexican *obrajes*, small manufacturers that used hand labor to make cloth, closed, leaving their former owners and employees in the streets. U.S. manufacturers competed with English manufacturers for the Mexican market.

Lucas Alamán, a Conservative in the Juárez government, argued in favor of developing Mexican manufacturing industries to replace the mining income lost to foreign interests. During his terms in government, Alamán worked to import industrial machinery and set up textile mills across Mexico. He advocated tariffs to protect Mexico's developing industries. The Liberal faction opposed tariffs, arguing for free trade. Neither policy seemed to work well.

When tariffs were high, British and U.S. merchants smuggled their goods into

Mexico. By smuggling, they avoided tariffs entirely. That meant less money collected by the government. In turn, less money was available for debt payments and public expenditures.

When tariffs were low, cheap imports cost less than Mexican textiles. Then Mexicans lost jobs and revenue. When Mexican workers were unemployed and Mexican businesses closed, then they could not pay taxes. Again, less money was available to the government for debt payments and public expenditures.

In October 1861, French, British, and Spanish leaders met in London and decided to invade Mexico, their strategy to occupy the customhouse at Veracruz. Veracruz was a key port city and its customhouse was a profitable center for collecting tariffs. This strategic position would enable the invaders to seize money for debt payments.

Mexico Is Conquered Again

When the foreign troops landed, President Benito Juárez tried to negotiate a settlement. France, however, wanted empire more than it wanted payments on the debts owed to it. Some Mexican monarchists had settled in France and convinced the French government that Mexico was

Liberal Victory

In History of Mexico, *Hubert Howe Bancroft describes the Liberals' victory and their continuing struggle.*

"The constitutionalists and reformers have won the victory. The power upheld by the reactionists during the last three years of horrors is overthrown. It would seem that Juárez and his fellow-laborers have a clear field, and an opportunity to plant the institutions to win which so many lives were sacrificed. But such is not the case. There are innumerable obstacles yet to overcome before reaching the happy consummation of their hopes.

The reactionary leaders though cast down are not crushed. Undismayed by reverses, they are still battling for supremacy under the war-cry, 'religion y fueros;' and to win they will resort to any device, even to inviting the intervention of European monarchies to their support. Nor is this the only difficulty the liberal administration has to contend with. Discordant elements among the liberals themselves must be harmonized, old standing abuses eradicated, and finances adjusted before the haven of safety is reached."

To increase industry in Mexico and to lessen debt owed to foreign banks, Lucas Alamán set up textile mills like this one all across the country.

ready to welcome a monarchy. The Spanish wife of Napoleon III, Empress Eugenia de Montijo, also promoted the cause of monarchy.

England and Spain, less interested in occupying Mexico, would not commit their troops to support a French cause. So a military victory was won solely by France, with French troops occupying Mexico City in 1863. President Juárez and a small group of close aides and government officials escaped toward the northern part of the country, and appealed to the United States for assistance. Now was the time to see whether the Monroe Doctrine could be used to help them. But mired in its own civil war, the United States was unable to offer much aid.

Conservatives in Mexico hoped that the French conquerors would reverse the reforms. They wanted the new rulers to give back church lands. The French, however, not only supported the reform laws, but also began to tax the rich and talk about equality for Indians. Although the French overthrew a Liberal government, their actions pleased Liberals more than they did Conservatives.

In 1864, the Archduke Maximilian, a descendant of the Austrian Hapsburg dynasty whose members ruled as dukes, emperors, kings, and princes in various European countries for more than six hundred years, arrived to become emperor of Mexico. His wife, a Belgian princess, became Empress Carlota. Under Maximilian's rule, France invested a lot of money in Mexico. British investors also returned. Emperor Maximilian returned the *ejidos* to the Indian villages that had owned them prior to dispersion. His government also tried to give more rights to workers.

One of Maximilian's new laws, for example, targeted hacienda owners and other employers by outlawing the beating of workers. These actions angered the Conservatives and the elite of Mexico, who wanted no limits on their power over workers.

Archduke Maximilian became the emperor of Mexico in 1864. His attempt to rule liberally pitted the conservatives and elites of Mexico against him.

Mexico for the Mexicans Again

While many Liberals approved of the French laws, they wanted a Mexican government under President Juárez. In 1866, threatened by European wars, Napoleon III called the French troops home. Without their protection, the emperor was in danger.

In addition, the American Civil War had ended the previous year, freeing the United States to send weapons and aid to the Liberal supporters of President Juárez. Mexicans who wanted to oust the foreign rulers and restore a Mexican republic under Mexican rule were known as Republicans. Both Liberal and Conservative Mexicans formed Republican armies and marched to overthrow the emperor. The Republicans defeated royalist troops at Querétaro, captured Emperor Maximilian and the two leading royalist generals, and executed all three on June 19, 1867.

Although President Juárez's term had ended in 1865, he remained self-proclaimed president during the two years of French rule and warfare, when elections could not be held. His opponent in the 1867 elections was a young general, Porfirio Díaz. Juárez won the election by a wide margin, and Porfirio Díaz retired to Oaxaca.

President Juárez granted amnesty to all of those who had fought on the side of the French. He demobilized the army and made peace with the church. He also made agreements with Mexico's creditors, so that they would not make war to collect debts again. Now at peace with the United States, Mexico agreed to settle claims of U.S. citizens against it. While President

Emperor Maximilian stands stoically during the final moments before his execution.

Juárez's government refused to pay any European loans made to Emperor Maximilian and the French conquerors, it agreed to make payments on debts to England. English investments in Mexico continued to be welcome. Mexico still had little capital for investment, and needed investments to rebuild after its wars.

Back in the presidency, Juárez continued what some call his most important contribution to Mexico—the establishment of public schools. Juárez believed in the value of education for all people.

While he had long promised to establish public schools, after the wars were over his dream was realized. Between 1857 and 1875, the number of public schools grew from 2,400 to 8,100.

The last obstacle to independence had been overcome. Never again would a foreign country be able to impose a king, emperor, or government on Mexico. Benito Juárez, an Indian, an elected president, and a Liberal reformer, had completed the struggle for independence begun by Miguel Hidalgo more than fifty years earlier.

8 Mexico in the World Today

Victory over the French secured Mexico's independence. Foreign countries no longer threatened its borders. But challenges still lay ahead.

The legacy of Mexico's War of Independence can be found in two themes: nationalism and equality. These themes were the basis of the War of Independence. Nationalism sparked the war with the United States over Texas and fueled Mexican resistance to the French and Emperor Maximilian. Equality was central to Miguel Hidalgo's army of independence and to La Reforma fifty years later. Both themes continue to resonate in Mexican political life in the twentieth century.

The End of Liberal Reforms

President Benito Juárez and his Liberal allies had been democratically elected to power again and again. As they dealt with the crises of civil war, foreign occupation, and economic collapse, however, the Liberals seemed less committed to their goals of equality and of a better life for campesinos (peasants) and workers. More and more, they focused simply on the problems of running the government and winning reelection.

Benito Juárez died in office in 1872, having served as president of Mexico for a total of fifteen years. His successor was his vice president and the head of the Mexican Supreme Court, Sebastián Lerdo de Tejada. Unlike President Juárez, Lerdo was not a popular leader.

Lerdo's antagonism to the Catholic Church was extreme. Though Juárez had limited the power of the church, he had been open to compromise. Not so Lerdo. His anticlericalism led him to forbid all religious parades or processions throughout the entire country. Great numbers of people loved the ritual processions, and were angered by his decision.

General Porfirio Díaz had opposed Juárez in the presidential elections of 1867 and 1871. After his second defeat, he began to organize discontented soldiers and former soldiers to revolt against the government. One of his slogans was "No Reelection," meaning that presidents should not be allowed to serve two consecutive terms.

The Porfiriato

In 1876, Díaz, supported by his personal army, took control of the government. In

Benito Juárez

In Maximilian and Juárez, *Jasper Ridley describes the poverty and isolation of the early life of Benito Juárez, the first Indian president of Mexico. His subsequent rise would be remarkable in any age.*

"Another hated liberal was the Indian Benito Juárez, who spoke only his tribal language, Zapotecan, until he was six or seven. He was born in a bamboo hut in the hamlet of San Pablo Guelatao, halfway up a mountain in the state of Oaxaca. Both his parents died before he was five, and he was brought up by his uncle, who taught him to speak Spanish and to read and write, for he thought the boy showed promise. The uncle threatened him with a severe beating if he was negligent in his studies, yet he intended that Benito should spend his life tending sheep on the hillside of Guelatao. So when Benito was twelve he decided to run away to his sister, who was a domestic servant in the city of Oaxaca.

On December 17, 1818, Juárez set out on foot over the mountains, determined to walk the forty miles to Oaxaca in one day, for it could be very cold at night, and the little mountain lions sometimes attacked children who slept on the hillside. At the top of the pass, he could look down on the valley of Oaxaca far below, and by nightfall he arrived at the house in the city where his sister worked. He was a very determined boy and would grow up to be a very determined man.

His sister was employed by a Creole merchant named Maza, who, impressed by Juárez's intelligence and character, arranged for him to stay with a Dominican monk in the city so that he could be educated for the Church. Juárez learned to speak Latin and French, but he was not attracted by the idea of becoming a priest, and his tutor, a broad-minded monk, sadly agreed that it would be better if Juárez became a lawyer."

Benito Juárez, the first Indian president of Mexico.

1877, he won an election for president and assumed virtually dictatorial powers. After amending the constitution to forbid re-election of a president, Díaz put a friend in office in 1880. His friend did such a bad job that Díaz had no trouble winning the 1884 election. He also had no trouble amending the constitution further to allow him to be reelected as often as he liked.

Díaz considered himself a liberal. Unlike Lerdo, he quickly made peace with the Catholic Church, but otherwise seemed to

Porfirio Díaz organized his own army to seize control of the government from Lerdo in 1876.

have few specific plans for government. Like Santa Anna forty years earlier, Porfirio Díaz was the kind of leader known as a caudillo. A caudillo is a strongman, sometimes but not always coming from the military. Díaz appointed government and military officials and expected the other branches of government to do pretty much as he wished. His power extended beyond government to other organizations in society. When Díaz took office, he quickly limited the freedom of the press. Some of his opponents were jailed and at least one was assassinated. Díaz said that he believed in democracy, but that it would only work with a highly developed people. Thus, he had no qualms about suppressing freedom and democracy in his own country. Supported by the military, Díaz held tightly to power for thirty-five years in a political era known as the Porfiriato.

From Porfiriato to Revolution

During the Porfiriato, Díaz promoted economic development. The Porfiriato built railroads, modernized mining, and developed the oil industry. Ownership of these industries and of other productive resources was still concentrated in the hands of the wealthy elite. Those who had been rich before the Juárez-Liberal reforms became even richer. They were joined by some Liberals made wealthy under Díaz and by foreign investors. Corruption was widespread.

Although economic development provided some new jobs, especially in mines, mills, and factories, the new jobs paid little.

Porfirio Díaz

Porfirio Díaz ruled as a caudillo. In A Concise History of Mexico from Hidalgo to Cárdenas, *Jan Bazant quotes extensively from Díaz to show his theory of government.*

"In the mind of Porfirio Díaz as well as of his collaborators, order and economic progress came to justify army rule. This of course brought in its wake a gradual restriction of the press which had been entirely free under Juárez and Lerdo. In fact, the press had been so free that it helped to undermine the regime of these two civilian presidents. Díaz had used this freedom in order to attain power but, knowing its corrosive effect, he justified its suppression on the ground that Mexico was not ready for it. In 1908, in the last years of his long rule, he declared 'democracy to be the one true, just principle of government, although in practice it is possible only among highly developed peoples.' These words, spoken in an interview with an American correspondent which was apparently intended for foreign consumption, remind us of similar words spoken by Iturbide and Santa Anna. 'Here in Mexico we have had different conditions,' Díaz continued; 'I received this government from the hands of a victorious army at a time when the people were divided and unprepared for the exercise of the extreme principles of democratic government. To have thrown upon the masses the whole responsibility of government at once would have produced conditions that might have discredited the cause of democracy.' And, 'we preserved the republican and democratic form of government. We defended the theory and kept it intact. Yet we adopted a patriarchal policy in the actual administration of national affairs, guiding and restraining popular tendencies, with full faith that an enforced peace would allow education, industry, and commerce to develop elements of stability and unity.'"

The vast majority of Mexicans were still either laborers or campesinos. They were still poor.

In late 1906, a financial crisis began to build. Strikes by workers demanding higher wages led to riots in which both

Emiliano Zapata, a farmer and village leader, championed the cause of land reform and workers' rights.

workers and supervisors were killed. Then the stock market collapsed. Factories laid off workers and many closed.

When workers rioted, the government sent in troops. The military killed several hundred people at a Rio Bolanco factory, and also executed local police who refused to fire on the crowd.

As economic collapse and unrest spread through the entire country, Díaz first announced retirement plans, then changed his mind. He jailed the candidate who ran against him for president in 1910. That candidate, Francisco Madero, escaped from jail, declared the 1910 elections null and void, and announced that he was assuming the presidency. He rallied a revolutionary army and entered Mexico City in triumph in June 1911. Díaz left Mexico and died in exile in Paris.

The Mexican Revolution

Now began the Mexican Revolution, ten years of war that devastated Mexico. This war had not two sides, but many. According to historian Jan Bazant, "The hungry ones fought for food, the landless for land, the wronged ones for redress of their grievance."[38] Alliances formed, shifted, broke apart.

Beside more traditional leaders, populist champions sprang up. A farmer and village leader named Emiliano Zapata spoke for the tenants, seasonal workers, and Indian people of the countryside. Without land of their own, they had been reduced to near slavery. Now they were ready to fight for their rights as human beings, and for the land they needed to live with dignity. Their voices echoed the theme of equality that had rallied Hidalgo's troops in the War of Independence.

U.S. president Woodrow Wilson landed troops in Veracruz in 1914. All sides united in opposing U.S. intervention, however, and the troops were withdrawn after six months. Opposition to foreign intervention—nationalism—was about the only point on which all sides could agree.

By 1917 a new government began to legislate reforms in the spirit of Hidalgo's dreams of justice and equality. The reforms, including return of *ejidos* to Indian villages, limits on the size of farms, legalization of strikes, and protections for workers, were written into law in the Constitution of 1917.

Nationalism was also part of the new government's plan. Foreign investors had taken over many of the country's mines. Now the government ordered that all underground resources belonged to Mexico. Mines and oil fields were part of the national heritage.

The new laws looked good on paper. In reality, change was harder to see. Agrarian reform moved very slowly. Land was simply not redistributed. Employers refused to raise wages. When workers went on strike, the government often forced them back to work. For Zapata, the reforms of 1917 were not enough. He swore that he would keep fighting until the poor of Mexico had land and justice, but was assassinated in 1919 by an officer in the Mexican army.

Peace remained a stranger to Mexico. Poor peasants knew that the promised reforms had not yet benefited them. Workers knew that the government still sided mostly with their employers. It would take yet another revolution to achieve more for Mexico.

Glossary

agrarian reform: Redistribution of farmland so that the people who live on the land can own it.

campesino: A poor farmer or farm laborer, often of Indian ancestry; a peasant.

caste: A social status acquired at birth, and usually impossible to change.

caudillo: A charismatic ruler, usually a military man and a dictator, whose strong personality wins the allegiance of many followers.

Centralist: Someone who believes in a strong central government.

class: A group of people sharing the same economic status and interests.

Creole: Someone of "pure" Spanish ancestry who was born in Mexico.

criollos letrados: The small group of well-educated Creoles who tried to head the revolution after the execution of Miguel Hidalgo.

egalitarian: Refers to a belief that all people should have equal social, economic, and political rights.

ejido: Land owned in common by a group of people, originally referring to land held in common by an Indian village.

elite: Small group of people at the top of society, by reason of wealth or land ownership or race or some other factor.

encomienda: A grant of land by the king of Spain, giving the *encomendero* the right to use the land and to use the labor of the Indians living on the land, while the king retains legal title.

Federalist: Someone who believes in a form of government that joins states together while leaving each state significant power to run its own affairs.

gachupines: Another name for *peninsulares*, or people born in Spain; some say that it means "those who wear spurs."

guerrilla warfare: A way of waging war that relies on stealthy attacks and quick retreats, small bands of fighters, and the support of the people.

hacienda: A large ranch or farm.

junta: A temporary governing board.

mercenary: A soldier for hire.

mestizo: A person of mixed Spanish and Indian ancestry.

monarchy: Rule by a king, queen, or emperor.

mulatto: A person of mixed black African and white European ancestry.

oligarchy: Government by a small, wealthy, powerful group of people.

peninsulares: People living in Mexico but born in Spain.

peon: A person living on an hacienda who does not own any land and is often in debt to the landowner.

Porfiriato: The political era when Porfirio Díaz ruled Mexico.

viceroy: The Spanish governor of New Spain sent by the Spanish king or queen.

Notes

Introduction: Independence and Justice: A Continuing Struggle

1.   L. Gutierrez de Lara and Edgcumb Pinchon, *The Mexican People: Their Struggle for Freedom.* Garden City, NY: Doubleday, Page, 1917, p. 51.

Chapter 1: Prelude: Conquest and Resistance

2.   James D. Henderson and Linda Roddy Henderson, *Ten Notable Women of Latin America.* Chicago: Nelson Hall, 1978, p. 3.

3.   Bernal Díaz del Castillo, *The Discovery and Conquest of Mexico.* Edited by Genaro García, translated by A. P. Maudslay. Introduction to the American edition by Irving A. Leonard. New York: Farrar, Straus & Giroux, 1956, p. 74.

4.   Ramón Eduardo Ruiz, *Triumph and Tragedy: A History of the Mexican People.* New York: W. W. Norton, 1992, p. 60.

5.   Ruiz, *Triumph and Tragedy*, p. 76.

6.   Quoted in Lewis Hanke, *Aristotle and the American Indians: A Study in Race Prejudice in the Modern World.* Bloomington: Indiana University Press, 1959, p. 47.

7.   Bartolomé de Las Casas, *The Devastation of the Indies, A Brief Account.* Translated by Herma Briffault. New York: Seabury Press, 1974, pp. 68–70.

Chapter 2: Father of Independence

8.   Ruiz, *Triumph and Tragedy*, p. 140.

9.   Arthur Howard Noll, *The Life and Times of Miguel Hidalgo y Costilla.* Chicago: A. C. McClurg, 1910, p. 33.

10.   Fay Robinson, *Mexico and Her Military Chieftains: From the Revolution of Hidalgo to the Present Time.* Hartford, CT: Silas Andrus & Son, 1848, p. 30.

11.   Noll, *The Life and Times of Miguel Hidalgo y Costilla*, pp. 68–70.

Chapter 3: El Grito de Dolores

12.   Ruiz, *Triumph and Tragedy*, pp. 131–32.

13.   Noll, *The Life and Times of Miguel Hidalgo y Costilla*, p. 76.

14.   Noll, *The Life and Times of Miguel Hidalgo y Costilla*, pp. 81–82.

15.   Robinson, *Mexico and Her Military Chieftains*, pp. 33–34.

16.   Noll, *The Life and Times of Miguel Hidalgo y Costilla*, p. 99.

17.   Noll, *The Life and Times of Miguel Hidalgo y Costilla*, p. 102.

18.   Hubert Howe Bancroft, *History of Mexico*, vol. IV. San Francisco: A. L. Bancroft, 1885, p. 290.

Chapter 4: Morelos and Iturbide Inherit the Revolution

19.   Robinson, *Mexico and Her Military Chieftains*, pp. 49–50.

20.   Jan Bazant, *A Concise History of Mexico from Hidalgo to Cárdenas.* London: Cambridge University Press, 1977, p. 22.

21.   Quoted in William Spence Robertson, *Iturbide of Mexico.* Durham, NC: Duke University Press, 1952, p. 14.

22.   Robertson, *Iturbide of Mexico*, p. 29.

23.   Quoted in Robertson, *Iturbide of Mexico*, p. 43.

24. Robinson, *Mexico and Her Military Chieftans*, p. 78.

25. Quoted in Robertson, *Iturbide of Mexico*, p. 111.

Chapter 5: Independence for Whom?

26. Quoted in Robertson, *Iturbide of Mexico*, p. 146.

27. Quoted in Robertson, *Iturbide of Mexico*, p. 192.

28. Bazant, *A Concise History of Mexico*, p. 43.

29. Ruiz, *Triumph and Tragedy*, p. 175.

30. Ruiz, *Triumph and Tragedy*, p. 176.

31. Ruiz, *Triumph and Tragedy*, p. 195.

Chapter 6: Texas and the Mexican-American War

32. Walter LaFeber, *Inevitable Revolutions: The United States in Central America.* New York: W. W. Norton, 1984, p. 19.

33. Ruiz, *Triumph and Tragedy*, p. 210.

34. Ruiz, *Triumph and Tragedy*, pp. 213–14.

Chapter 7: Debt and War

35. Ruiz, *Triumph and Tragedy*, p. 231.

36. Ruiz, *Triumph and Tragedy*, p. 232.

37. Ruiz, *Triumph and Tragedy*, p. 237.

Chapter 8: Mexico in the World Today

38. Bazant, *A Concise History of Mexico*, p. 141.

For Further Reading

James D. Atwater and Ramón E. Ruiz, *Out from Under: Benito Juárez and Mexico's Struggle for Independence.* Garden City, NY: Doubleday, 1969. This biography of Benito Juárez sets his life story in the context of the War of Independence, which began a few years after his birth. Nearly half of the book focuses on the War of Independence. Written for young people.

Jan Gleiter and Kathleen Thompson, *Miguel Hidalgo y Costilla.* Austin, TX: Raintree Publishers/Steck-Vaughn, 1989. A biography of the revolutionary priest, written for children.

Mary Ellen Jones, ed., *Christopher Columbus and His Legacy: Opposing Viewpoints.* San Diego, CA: Greenhaven Press, 1992. A title in the Opposing Viewpoints series, this book presents essays from modern and historical sources that take opposing positions on Christopher Columbus, the conquistadores, and the Indians of the Americas. Excellent resource.

John David Ragan, *Emiliano Zapata.* New York: Chelsea House, 1989. Biography of the revolutionary leader Emiliano Zapata, who, a century after the War of Independence, led the Mexican Revolution. Written for young people.

Rebecca Stefoff, *Independence and Revolution in Mexico: 1810–1940.* New York: Facts On File, 1993. This book presents the grand sweep of Mexican history from the War of Independence through the Mexican Revolution. It offers especially good integration of cultural history from the poetry of Sor Juana to the art of Diego Rivera and Frida Kahlo. Written for young people.

Frank de Varona, *Benito Juárez: President of Mexico.* Brookfield, CT: Gallin House Press, 1993. Illustrated biography of Benito Juárez, president of Mexico and leader of the Liberal reforms. Easy reading for young people.

———, *Miguel Hidalgo y Costilla: Father of Mexican Independence.* Brookfield, CT: Millbrook Press, 1993. Illustrated biography of Miguel Hidalgo gives substantial information about the setting of the War of Independence. Easy reading for young people.

Works Consulted

Books

Lucas Alamán, *Historia de Méjico, desde los primeros movimientos que prepararon su independencia en el año de 1808 hasta la época presente*. Mexico: J. M. Lara, 1850. This multivolume work was written by a Mexican aristocrat and political leader who participated in many of the events of the War of Independence. The history is entirely in Spanish, and makes quite difficult reading, as the idioms and syntax are 150 years old.

Ramón Alcáraz et al., *The Other Side or Notes for the History of the War Between Mexico and the United States*. Translated from the Spanish by Albert Ramsey. New York: John Wiley, 1850. A history of the war between Mexico and the United States "from the other side," that is, from the point of view of Mexico. This book gives valuable background on the situation in Mexico during the first half of the nineteenth century.

Hubert Howe Bancroft, *History of Mexico*. Vol. IV. San Francisco: A. L. Bancroft, 1885. A well-documented, scholarly account of Mexican history by a U.S. historian, writing in the nineteenth century.

Jan Bazant, *A Concise History of Mexico from Hidalgo to Cárdenas*. London: Cambridge University Press, 1977. A modern, scholarly history of Mexico, written by one of the preeminent twentieth-century scholars of Mexican history.

Leslie Bethell, ed., *Mexico Since Independence*. Cambridge, England: Cambridge University Press, 1991. Includes articles by various Mexico scholars previously published as parts of Volumes III, V, and VII of the *Cambridge History of Latin America*. "From Independence to the Liberal Republic, 1821–1867" by Jan Bazant is most relevant to the War of Independence.

Howard Cline, *The United States and Mexico*. 1953. Reprint, New York: Atheneum, 1966. Originally published as a volume in the American Foreign Policy Library, this book includes a brief history of Mexico as well as more extended discussion of U.S.-Mexico relations since independence.

Bernal Díaz del Castillo, *The Discovery and Conquest of Mexico*. Edited by Genaro García, translated by A. P. Maudslay. Introduction to the American edition by Irving A. Leonard. New York: Farrar, Straus & Giroux, 1956. Classic first-hand story of the conquistadores' arrival in Mexico, written by a lower-ranking member of Cortes's army. This book, which remains in print in more than one translation, was one of the first published historical accounts written by someone from the lower ranks of society.

Juan Friede and Benjamin Keen, eds., *Bartolomé de las Casas in History*. Dekalb: Northern Illinois University Press, 1971. Scholarly compilation of essays on the significance of Bartolomé de Las Casas, his writings, and his place in history.

Kevin Gosner, *Soldiers of the Virgin*. Tucson: University of Arizona Press, 1992.

Focusing on a little-known part of Mexican history, anthropologist Kevin Gosner meticulously documents and analyzes Indian rebellions under the banner of the Blessed Virgin prior to the time of independence.

L. Gutierrez de Lara and Edgcumb Pinchon, *The Mexican People: Their Struggle for Freedom*. Garden City, NY: Doubleday, Page, 1917. This book, written during the Mexican Revolution by a committed socialist and revolutionary, gives a passionate and opinionated description of the War of Independence.

Lewis Hanke, *All Mankind Is One: A Study of the Disputation Between Bartolomé de Las Casas and Juan Ginés de Sepúlveda on the Religious and Intellectual Capacity of the American Indians*. Dekalb: Northern Illinois University Press, 1974. Modern scholarly analysis of the debate between Bartolomé de Las Casas and Juan Sepúlveda regarding colonialism and specifically regarding their argument over whether or not Indians are human beings.

———, *Aristotle and the American Indians: A Study in Race Prejudice in the Modern World*. Bloomington: Indiana University Press, 1959. Academic discussion of the history of race prejudice, including analysis of the views of Aristotle as used to justify European domination of the American Indians during the colonial period and beyond.

James D. Henderson and Linda Roddy Henderson, *Ten Notable Women of Latin America*. Chicago: Nelson Hall, 1978. Modern biography focusing on ten significant women in Latin American history, including biographies of two Mexican women, Malinche and Sor Juana Inés de la Cruz. The book sheds light on the situation of women in Mexico during early colonial times.

Walter LaFeber, *Inevitable Revolutions: The United States in Central America*. New York: W. W. Norton, 1984. An eminent historian of U.S. foreign policy does not focus directly on Mexico in this study, but does describe the origins of U.S. foreign policy toward all of Latin America.

Bartolomé de Las Casas, *The Devastation of the Indies, A Brief Account*. Translated by Herma Briffault. New York: Seabury Press, 1974. Las Casas, a Spanish priest, participated in the colonization of the Americas, but later condemned the inhumane treatment of the Indians by the Spaniards. This book is both a first-person testimony and a polemic against the Spanish colonial system.

Michael C. Meyer and William L. Sherman, *The Course of Mexican History*. 4th ed. New York: Oxford University Press, 1991. Up-to-date, interesting, and informative history of Mexico, with substantial description of the War of Independence and extensive documentation and bibliographic citation.

Robert P. Millon, *Zapata: The Ideology of a Peasant Revolutionary*. New York: International Press, 1968. Account of the political life of the revolutionary leader Emiliano Zapata, who, a century after the War of Independence, led the Mexican Revolution.

Arthur Howard Noll, *The Life and Times of Miguel Hidalgo y Costilla*. Chicago: A. C. McClurg, 1910. A well-documented biography of the priest-revolutionary that also describes the social and historical setting in which he lived.

Miguel Ramos de Arizpe, *Report That Dr. Miguel Ramos de Arizpe, Priest of Borbon, and Deputy in the Present General and Special Cortes of Spain for the Province of Coahuila One of the Four Eastern Interior Provinces of the Kingdom of Mexico Presents to the August Congress.* Translated by Nettie Lee Benson. Austin: University of Texas Press, 1950. This report, sympathetic to Mexico and Mexicans, was written in 1812 by a Spanish official delegated to investigate the situation of the colony and report back to the government of Spain about the conditions in Mexico. Written just at the beginning of the War of Independence, the report gives a good picture of colonial Mexico.

Jasper Ridley, *Maximilian and Juárez.* New York: Ticknor & Fields, 1992. Fascinating personal background on leading figures from the War of Independence through the Liberal reforms of Benito Juárez in the mid–nineteenth century. With the concern for psychosocial factors that became quite common in the late twentieth century, Ridley draws connections between early life experiences of these leaders and their later political convictions.

William Spence Robertson, *Iturbide of Mexico.* Durham, NC: Duke University Press, 1952. This scholarly biography of the man who finally led Mexico to independence from Spain includes significant description of the impact of Mexican independence on other countries in the region and on Spanish colonialism in general.

Fay Robinson, *Mexico and Her Military Chieftains: From the Revolution of Hidalgo to the Present Time.* Hartford, CT: Silas Andrus & Son, 1848. A lively, opinionated, passionate account of some of Mexico's leaders. Though clearly subjective, the narrative is both personal and highly readable.

William Davis Robinson, *Memoirs of the Mexican Revolution.* Philadelphia: Lydia H. Bailey, 1820. This is a sympathetic, first-person account of the Mexican War of Independence by a U.S. citizen who, like a modern reporter, relates vivid details of the War of Independence.

James D. Rudolph, *Mexico: A Country Study.* Washington, DC: GPO, 1985. This official government publication gives a capsule history of Mexico, as well as information and statistics on modern-day Mexico.

Ramón Eduardo Ruiz, *Triumph and Tragedy: A History of the Mexican People.* New York: W. W. Norton, 1992. Modern Mexico scholar, widely published in both Spanish and English translation, gives a well-documented and readable overview of the history of Mexico, from the Indian civilizations prior to the arrival of Cortés to the late twentieth century.

Earl H. Swanson, Warwick Bray, and Ian Farrington, *The Ancient Americas.* New York: Peter Bedrick Books, 1989. Illustrated description of the tribes, nations, languages, and cultures of the Americas, from twenty thousand years ago to the fifteenth century. Prepared by archaeologists and other scholars, the book, one in a series called The Making of the Past, includes sections on the Mayan, Aztec, and other Mexican Indian cultures.

Herman J. Viola and Carolyn Margolis, *Seeds of Change.* Washington, DC: Smithsonian Institution Press, 1991. Published as a quincentennial commemoration of Columbus's arrival in the Americas, this lavishly illustrated book contains descriptions of various aspects of Indian life in the Americas and the impact of European contact.

Jack Weatherford, *Indian Givers.* New York: Ballantine Books, 1988. An anthropologist's account of the contributions of Indians to modern civilization and culture in the areas of government, medicine, agriculture, architecture, and ecology. Includes significant information on early Mayan and Aztec civilizations.

G. B. Winton, *Mexico, Past and Present.* Nashville, TN: Cokesbury Press, 1928. Colorful and sympathetic history of Mexico from Indian times to the Mexican Revolution, written by an American "to make our next-door neighbors better known" in the United States.

Howard Zinn, *A People's History of the United States.* New York: Harper & Row, 1980. A historian's well-documented account of U.S. history from a popular rather than official perspective. Includes a brief section on the conquest of Mexico by Cortés.

Periodical

"Guerrilla Uprising in Chiapas," *Centroamérica,* January 1994.

Index

Credits